Drawn With Loving Kindness

Adriene R. Dallas

Drawn With Loving Kindness by Adriene R. Dallas

Scripture quotations marked NLT are taken from the Holy Bible, New Living Translation, copyright 1996, 2004. Used by permission of Tyndale House Publishers, Inc., Wheaton, Illinois 60189. All rights reserved.

Scripture taken from the HOLY BIBLE, NEW INTERNATIONAL VERSION®. Copyright © 1973, 1978, 1984 International Bible Society. Used by permission of Zondervan. All rights reserved.

Scripture quotations taken from the Amplified® Bible, Copyright © 1954, 1958, 1962, 1964, 1965, 1987 by The Lockman Foundation Used by permission." (www.Lockman.org)

Adriene R. Dallas
Visit my website at www.livingwatersbooks.com

Printed in the United States of America

First Printing: December 2008

ISBN-13:978-15-59581-475-3
ISBN-10:1-59581-475-2

PUBLISHED BY:
BRENTWOOD CHRISTIAN PRESS
4000 BEALLWOOD AVENUE
COLUMBUS, GEORGIA 31904

Table Of Contents

Foreword

Mr. Eric L. Jones

"To everything there is a season and a time to every purpose under the heaven." Surely, Adriene is coming into her season. She has taken the word of God and made it flesh. Through the years of knowing the relationship between her and my wife, I can only say, "When I think about the goodness of my Lord and Saviour Jesus Christ, I'm reminded about my sister in Christ...Adriene." She is a living witness of the LOVE the Holy Scriptures speaks to us all. Her writings have led me through the scriptures to increase my awareness of the true meaning of the First Covenant Relationship: Marriage.

Adriene's title, *Drawn With Loving Kindness,* keeps my thoughts flowing through my mind while the Holy Spirit examines the reason and intent of the heart. Her writings reflect the root cause of divorce and bring alive the true meaning of marriage. Adriene consistently brings to life individuals who are depicted in scriptures and reminds us that we are human just as they were so long ago. With our fears, jealousy, envy, strife, disappointments, trials, and tribulations, she brings human feelings into focus and to the root cause of divorce. My wife and I have never been divorced, but surely the chapter, "Are You Thinking about It" has crossed my mind in our thirty-six years of marriage.

Adriene's insight into the Holy Scriptures delivers the very depths of God's heart towards marriage and divorce. In her writings, Adriene challenges each individual to seek the Lord first before an outcome has been decided upon for any drastic life change. Many times in marriage discontent, we ask ourselves questions such as "Should I leave my spouse?" and "When is enough, enough?" Her guided writings probe the beliefs that we have grown up with those questions, which in themselves may be contrary to the word of God. With that in mind, we make unwise decisions when we fail to realize that everybody has sinned and come short of the glory of God.

Adriene has put her life to pin and ink for the world to see; in her musings, people's lives have been changed to choose life rather than death. The love that she has turns the pages of my mind to the realization of the truths that God will have his people believe concerning marriage and divorce. Upon reflection of my sister's divorce, I am empowered by Adriene's words that pinpoint the inspired word of God and that bring those scriptures to the table for my dining pleasure (smile). Oh, taste and see that the Lord is good. Surely Adriene is reaching for the good part of life despite the downfalls that have come her way, and through her words, people's lives are changed.

Through her trials and many disappointments, Adriene is the living witness of a virtuous woman. She has been divorced and may have strayed from her beliefs. However, through many countless conversations into the wee hours of the morning, my sister in Christ has come full circle from divorce to a right relationship with Jesus Christ. Adriene will continue to do good and not evil all the days of her life. She is like the virtuous woman that is written of in the book of Proverbs.

Her first book speaks from the depths of her soul to communicate to those individuals who may have gone through a divorce or who are thinking about it. Nevertheless, her writings continue to touch the very core of the first covenant marriage that the Holy Scriptures teaches to those who read its message. Her book has gone even deeper to the very depths of my own belief and brings my spirit to a surface that has not been tapped through the ages of time.

Through many long phone conversations, she still rises up early to reconsider the thoughts of her Lord and Saviour Jesus Christ. Each trial and tribulation has christened her mind, body, and soul to the heights that the Lord will have her do with her writing gift. She considers a field, divorce, and plants a vineyard, her writing, to bring mankind to the knowledge of a realm as shown in *Drawn With Loving Kindness*. Through her own perceived thoughts, Adriene continues to gird her loins with strength. She layeth her hands to write while, at the same time, she stretches her hands toward the poor and needy in spirit.

My sister is not afraid of the coldness of her surroundings for her writings are clothed with righteousness. Her covering is of the Holy Spirit and in that are her strength and power to make changes in people's lives and marriage. She continues to open her mouth in wisdom, and in her tongue is the law of kindness. When she consider the lilies of the field and the many desperate times that divorce has caused to the root of God's example, Adriene continues to allow the Holy Ghost to have the mind of Christ in her writings. People who have allowed divorce to come between them and their marriages should listen as the words of this book speak to the very depths of their bowels. *Drawn with Loving Kindness* is truly an inspired book raising questions and giving answers to challenge the inner person not to choose divorce.

Very respectfully,

Eric L. Jones
Your Brother in Christ

Foreword

Reverend Phyllis Brantley

From the moment I met Adriene Dallas I knew something was different about the lady. It wasn't that she was spiritual or religious it had more to do with the way she looks at you and smiles as though she has a secret. I never quite understood what the look of secrecy was until I read her first book "Psst! Are you Divorced? Are you Thinking About It?"... By this time I had matured in my faith in Christ Jesus so when I opened the book I knew that the words on the page were true revelations from God and that He had begun to share, to reveal the secret to Adriene to be shared throughout the world. At this time I had been married for over 25 years, never been divorced nor thinking of it, yet from the power of the anointing of the revealed Word to Adriene, I received it and was inspired to increase my Faith in the reconciliation of the first covenant relationship. That is what I love about Adriene's belief, you don't have to be where she is to eat from this delightful table of the abundance of God's Word. He uses Adriene's belief to help you believe.

When Adriene made me aware of "Drawn with Loving Kindness" I smiled and thought how many years has it been since God shared this wonderful, powerful secret with Adriene, at that moment the Holy Spirit spoke to me and said "it's not a secret any longer it's a call to a Promise from God." Adriene has a Promise from God that in His Power He is so abundant He will take our everyday thoughts and way of focusing on hurts, disappointments, loneliness, pain and He will remind us of His matchless power of love. In almost every conversation with Adriene I am reminded of a woman that lacks the ability to lean on her own understanding. She truly reminds me of the Hebrews 11:6 "But without Faith it is impossible to please him: for he that cometh to God must believe that he is, and that he is a rewarder of them that diligently seek him." That's why Noah built a boat even when there had never been any rain on the earth; that's why Abraham left all that he knew not knowing where he was to go, that's why Sarah after laughing to herself received physical power to conceive a child when she was long past the age to do so.

You see what Adriene does for us in this modern day, is to help us believe in God's ability to do what He promises He will do no matter how long it takes. This writing of love is more than a book to "help" us hold on this writing is the promise of God! To be able to truly walk in the promise of God you can not lean on your own understanding. You must "lack your own common sense" so to speak. Please understand this, Adriene Dallas believes God, she believes his promises, but her life's mission is MORE than about His promise to her it is about her promise to Him.

The promise to trust Him no matter what the dark clouds may say. To walk in the knowledge that the more she grows the more He trusts and reveals and this great revelation is All about His Glorious keeping Power in all situations of the this affliction. The Keeping power of finding joy in the midst of sorrow, peace in deep troubled waters, friendship in the dark lonely hours and contentment in knowing that you are on this great journey for the Kingdom agenda and that He counts you Faithful to endure. So in enduring she has lived a life for Him with Him, dreaming, seeing, trusting, growing, walking and most of all reaching out to countless men and women, showing through her situation that anything and all things are possible. If you only believe!

You see Adriene has learned in her Faith that God is able and all we must do is trust and believe. As we go on this journey with Adriene she takes the Word of God and salvation comes, character develops and friendships are restored. It is more than a marriage book. It is a book about God's love shared through my sister that is faithful to her Promise to Him. I truly believe Adriene will one day meet the Elders of Faith, I want to be there with her to receive that promise in glory. I say "sister" march on. Believe God. Help us to believe God. This book *is* for every believer.

To the Faithful
Reverend Phyllis Brantley

Preface

A Credible Witness Against
the Prosecutor

If you have not had an opportunity to read my first book, *Psst! Are you Divorced? Are you Thinking About It?,* please allow me this time to tell you why this divorced woman is a credible witness against the prosecutor and an excellent witness for the Restoration of the First Covenant Relationship – Marriage.

First, because I am divorced I can firmly say: if you are divorced, and right now the desire of your heart is to live alone for the rest of your life; or you are married and you are considering divorce; you don't mean this. Let me show you in the Word of God what you should desire.

Your desire should be to please the Father. And in pleasing Him, you will find seeking His will, way and purpose for your life to be the most important thing you could do. And when I sought after Him, the Holy Spirit led me to First Corinthians, chapter 7, verse 11: "*But and if she depart, let her remain unmarried, or be reconciled to her husband: and let not the husband put away his wife.*"

When the verse was first revealed to me all I wanted to know was, "Okay God, how do I live the rest of my life alone?" As you can see, I was only thinking how impossible it would be to reconcile with my former spouse. At that point in my life I was not willing to consider reconciliation. Too much hurt and betrayal had come between us. Then the Holy Spirit showed me, me.

The Holy Spirit taught me again those things that should have been evident in my character. He showed me areas in my life that should have been producing much fruit. Through his teaching, the Holy Spirit led me to ten narrow gates called: love, joy, peace, longsuffering, gentleness, goodness, faith, meekness, temperance, and oh yes, *forgiveness.* And at each gate the Holy Spirit gave me an opportunity to choose to go after the high call-

9

ing and follow after Christ. Or, I could choose to go my own way by not entering the narrow gates. I could choose to either turn towards God or choose to turn away from Him.

But I knew I had received Jesus Christ as my Lord and Savior. Where was I to go? I knew that only the Lord has the words for eternal life. Faced with this revelation, I allowed the Holy Spirit to lead me into all truth. God calls divorce a curse. When Jesus died on the cross at Calvary, He redeemed us from the curse of divorce too. Since that day of revelation, the Holy Spirit has built up my faith so much so that I believe God for the restoration of the first covenant relationship – marriage!

Over time I learned to take my focus off of reconciling with my spouse, but to focus on seeking first the kingdom of God and His righteousness, and then all these things shall be added unto me. As my faith grew for the restoration of the first covenant relationship, my fruit (character) began to get squeezed. I have to tell you there were many times when I did not like having my character (fruit) squeezed. But a dear friend helped me by saying this "*squeezing is the only way to get the juice, or anointing out of you*". It is so funny how the simplest of things made the most profound impressions and changes in my character and in my spirit. Let me share another example. This is a story about a rich man who was cast into hell.

> **Luke 16:27-31 KJV** Then he said, I pray thee therefore, father, that thou wouldest send him to my father's house: For I have five brethren; that he may testify unto them, lest they also come into this place of torment. Abraham saith unto him, They have Moses and the prophets; let them hear them. And he said, Nay, father Abraham: but if one went unto them from the dead, they will repent. And he said unto him, If they hear not Moses and the prophets, neither will they be persuaded, though one rose from the dead.

I identify with the rich man who was left begging for a cool drop of water. And because I identify with him, I believe that I am a credible witness against Satan, the prosecutor. Divorce is a curse and a type of hell! **And this hell is an awful place of torment. You cannot mean you want to come here too.**

Father, if I cannot have a drop of cool water, then Lord, send me to warn my brothers and sisters who are married and thinking about divorce. Let me warn them of the curses to come if they fail to resist the temptations and deceptions that lead to divorce. And send me to those who are now divorced. Let me go encourage and comfort them; by reminding them that NOTHING, (which includes the restoration of the first covenant relationship – marriage) is impossible for you Lord.

A Special Thanks and Acknowledgement to Kenneth O. Dallas Sr.

For giving me permission to release this next testament of the goodness, the grace, and the tender mercies of our Lord.

Dedication

This book is dedicated to the lost sheep of the house of Israel *(Matthew 10:6)*. I also dedicate this book to my son Byron and his wife Jennifer; teach your children and my great-grandchildren how to honor and treasure their First Covenant Relationship *(Deuteronomy 4:9)*.

Chapter 1

Drawn With Loving Kindness

When I finished the last chapter of my book, *Psst! Are you Divorced? Are You Thinking About It?*, I knew I had moved into a new season. In this new season I began to understand that it would be according to my faith how I would come into God's promises.

I did not know where the Lord was leading me. I only knew destiny was beckoning me. I knew I had to keep moving forward in faith. I had to pursue the purpose for my call.

Notes from my Journal
25 June 2005

Father, how will your word be made manifest? I heard in my spirit, *"Yea, I have loved thee with an everlasting love: there with lovingkindness have I drawn thee."* **Jeremiah 31:3** *You too can draw others with loving kindness."* And I also heard, "Love bears all things, believes all things, hopes all things, endures all things. Love never fails." **1 Corinthians 13:7-8 NLT** As I considered what I had heard and remembered, I began to understand I would need to show by faith and by my works that love never fails.

Today, I embrace my purpose. When I look back over the past few years since I released my first book; I often pause and reflect on the people I have met. People, whom I truly believe the Lord, sent me by your way. I know that I was not placed in your path by accident. My path was redirected to give you an answer to your question.

Whether the story I told was pure wonderment, a curiosity, or hard to believe, time and time again testimonies would come back how the Father had indeed reconciled His people to Him. There are amazing testimonies how the Father has restored relationships, marriages, and ultimately how the Father has brought together whole families. For this I bless the Lord. Each testimony is another witness to God's love, faithfulness, goodness and mercy towards His people!

Restoring the first covenant relationship will not be easy. But be encouraged. Don't quit now. Don't give up now. Restoring the first covenant relationship requires that we learn to be patient and diligent through process and time. **The Promise:** *"The glory of this latter house shall be greater than of the former, saith the LORD of hosts: and in this place will I give peace, saith the LORD of hosts."* **Haggai 2:9**

To fully understand process and time, we need a pattern. The pattern set before me, is the biblical account of a virtuous woman. The woman I am speaking of is Sarah, Abraham's wife. To me Sarah is the personification of most women. She was a wise business woman with strength of character, with inward and outer beauty, grace, and yes, Sarah, she had her issues.

The bible tells us Sarah reverenced her husband, Abraham. I believe it must have grieved Sarah that she was barren and was not able to bear children for her husband. It must have grieved Sarah terribly, to hear her husband tell the Lord, he, Abraham, could not have children. **Genesis 15:2** Abraham speaking to God, "...seeing I go childless".

Sarah had another issue. Sarah was an eavesdropper. She was eavesdropping when she overheard an angel tell Abraham he would be the father of many nations. When she heard the promise Sarah scoffed and laughed at the very idea. **Genesis 18:10, 12** And Sarah heard it in the tent door, which was behind him [Abraham]. There fore Sarah laughed within herself, saying, After I am waxed old shall I have pleasure, my lord being old also?

I also believe that Sarah was there when her husband left their tent at night, and watched him as he meditated on the promises of God. Abraham had to be outside when according to: **Genesis 15:5-**

6 ...and (the angel) said, Look now toward heaven, and tell the stars, if thou be able to number them: and he said unto him, So shall thy seed be. And he (Abraham) believed in the Lord....

Women, be honest, what would you say, or think, if your husband suddenly looked like he was going somewhere...at night? Knowing me, I would ask him, "Where are you going this late at night?" What if your husband answered by saying; "I am just going out for a little walk." Well speaking for myself, I would have drawn back the curtain to watch and see where my husband was going. I would have been found peeking and straining to see and hear.

Fourteen years went by, and every night Sarah must have watched as Abraham left the tent. From her secret position, Sarah could hear Abraham rehearse over and over the promise that he would be the father of many nations; **Genesis 22:17** That in blessing I will bless thee, and in multiplying I will multiply thy seed as the stars of the heaven, and as the sand which is upon the seashore;.... And year after barren year I believe Sarah would grieve all the more.

Sarah desperately wanted to give Abraham children that she did what "women" do; she felt the pressure of time. Because Sarah was old, [**Genesis 18:11**], she compromised on the promise and went to Abraham with her solution to a present situation.

> **Genesis 16:2** And Sarai said unto Abram, Behold now, the Lord hath restrained me from bearing: I pray thee, go in unto my maid; it may be that I may obtain children by her.

Then when Sarah's handmaid found out she was pregnant with Abraham's child, she began to despise her mistress. **Genesis 16:5** And Sarai said unto Abram, [*my bad*] be upon thee: I have given my maid into thy bosom; and when she saw that she had conceived, I was despised in her eyes: the Lord judge between me and thee. Verse 6 ...And when Sarai dealt hardly with her [Hagar], she [Hagar] fled from her [Sarai's] face.

Sarah was all woman. Sarah loved her husband, so much she was willing to do anything for Abraham, so she thought. Husbands and wives, the moral of this story is: the situation will get out of control when another person is brought into your marriage, especially your bedroom.

Because of jealously, Sarah forced Hagar into the desert, but God sent the now pregnant Hagar back to Abraham's camp. **Genesis 16:11** "Behold, thou art with child,...."

> **Genesis 16:9** And the angel of the Lord said unto [Hagar], Return to thy mistress, and submit thyself under her hands.

Now isn't that interesting? What would you do if God sent someone you thought was out of your life back into your life? When Hagar returned, she must have told her mistress and Abraham what the angel of the Lord had said. Based on this information, Hagar was allowed to live in Abraham's camp for fourteen years. For fourteen years Sarah submitted to God's commandment to Hagar. Hagar and Ishmael lived with Abraham and Sarah for fourteen years before Isaac, the son of promise was born. **Genesis 17:21, and 25**. The angel of the Lord said Isaac would be born "in the next year". *Ishmael was thirteen years old at the time the angel made this declaration.*

After Isaac was born, and he was eight days old, Abraham made a great feast in honor of the Hebrew tradition of circumcision. During the course of the celebration Sarah saw Ishmael mock Isaac, [*in effect, Ishmael was blaspheming the work of the Holy Spirit[1]*]. Sarah pleaded with Abraham to send Hagar and Ishmael away, but Abraham was grieved because of the boy. Then God spoke to Abraham, and permitted Abraham to send Hagar and Ishmael away. **Genesis 21:12** God said, "...for in Isaac thy seed be called."

Another thing I observed was how Sarah submitted to her husband. Sarah completely trusted Abraham even when he sold her to Pharaoh, just to save his soul.

Genesis 12:12-13,15-16 Therefore it shall come to pass when the Egyptians shall see thee, [Sarah was very beautiful young men desired her] that they shall say, This is his wife: and they will kill me, but they will save thee alive. Say, I pray thee, thou are my sister: that it may be well with me for thy sake; and my soul shall live because of thee. ....and the woman [Sarah] was taken into Pharaoh's house. And he [Pharaoh] entreated Abram well for her sake; and he had sheep, and oxen, and he asses, and menservants, and maidservants, and she asses, and camels.

1Peter 3:1-2 Likewise, ye wives be in subjection to your own husbands; that, if any obey not the word, thy also may without the word be won by the conversations of the wives: While they behold your chaste conversation coupled with fear.

1Peter 3:6 New Living Translation (NLT) For instance Sarah obeyed her husband, Abraham, when she called him her master. You are her daughters when you do what is right without fear of what your husbands might do.

A Note From My Journal
7 August 2002

On the day of our appointment at the divorce court, my husband said he was surprised to see me there. I told him I had to be there. I told him that in the twinkling of an eye God could touch his heart and we could leave this place still husband and wife. He said even though he was fifty-one percent sure "this – the divorce" was the wrong decision for us, he was still going through with it. I then said; "I am your wife. And as your wife, I will stand with you in any decision you make as the head of our household." I told him, as his wife even if the roof was on fire, the house was burning, and everything was shaking and crashing down upon us, I would still stand with him.

In August 2002, I had the right to accept the world's facts concerning the death of my marriage. But the Holy Spirit exhorted me to believe that God's word is true. I was called to pray for reconciliation, and I did. On March 28, 2006, the seed that was sown in the spirit realm on August 7, 2002 sprouted its first blade. **James 5:16** The effectual fervent prayer of a righteous man availeth much. Prayer works!

Yes, today I am still divorced. In, **1 Corinthians 7:10,11**, it says, "And unto the married I command, *yet not I, but the Lord*, Let not the wife depart from her husband. But and if she depart let her remain unmarried or be reconciled to her husband."

On 7 August 2002, I did not understand why this scripture was being illuminated. But under the light of "*Nothing Is Impossible For God*" I caught the revelation of **1 Corinthians 7:11.** God calls me [meaning He still does] "wife". If God is the same yesterday, today, and forever, and He is, then God never changed His mind concerning the first covenant relationship. In every single divorce, and there are no exceptions, it was either the husband or the wife, or both who changed their minds concerning their covenant relationship. But God never changed His mind since the day He stood witness to our covenant relationship - marriage.

Believe me, there I was asking again, "Father, I do not understand. What is it that you are trying to get me to hear, to understand, and to do?" Was I really being asked to lean not to my own understanding? Yes. Was I being really asked if I would just believe God, and yield to the Holy Spirit, He the Father could move in and through my life? Yes.

It absolutely amazes me; the God of all creation was asking me to trust Him! He certainly did not have to, but He oh so very kindly and gently asked me to just believe Him, to trust in Him.

Wow...just thinking about that moment still moves me. Yes, in that moment, I was willing to give up my understanding of what was logical for what the Holy Spirit would bring me into.

Hebrews 11:6 But without faith it is impossible to please him; for he that cometh to God must believe that he is, and that he is a rewarder of them that diligently seek him.

I guess I kind of knew on some level what the Lord would bring me into would take time, as I went through the process. But I did not have at that time a full measure of what process and time really meant. I did not have at the time a complete understanding of how much the journey would exact from my mind, my heart and my soul. Now I look back at all of the dying to my selfish timeline and my selfish desires that I had to do. I had to first bury me, so that I could live in Christ.

I proved that I did not have a full concept of process and time when I became frustrated with my husband when I said I was sorry, and I was ignored. I even apologized for things I did or was slack to do as a wife; but he did not hear me or respond positively to me. I even repented to God of my sins. Unfortunately, the decisions I made in my marriage had created too many "crooked ways".

I was too late in noticing the seriousness of my actions or my inaction. I was too late in my attempts to fix my mistakes. I had lost all credibility with my husband. The seeds I sowed in my marriage were indeed "crooked ways". Only the Father could make my ways straight. **Isaiah 40:4** Every valley shall be exalted, and every mountain and hill shall be made low: and the crooked shall be made straight, and the rough places plain:

I knew that I could not fix what was wrong between my husband and me. Our marriage was over; and I had helped. Believe me, my attention was held captive. It is so true. You don't miss your water until your well runs dry. I was entering a very dry place.

Ringing in my ear was, **Matthew 6:33** But seek ye first the kingdom of God and His righteousness, and all these things shall be added unto you. I yielded to the Holy Spirit's breaking and making. During that season of my life I purposely set myself apart. I needed to hear the Holy Spirit clearly. I had to sit quietly to study and learn. I had to get an understanding of what was being spoken into my life. In that moment I transitioned into my next phase; observing seed time and harvest.

Observing seed time and harvest also helped me understand there is a reason for going through process and time. **Lesson learned:** restoring the first covenant relationship will not happen over night. I had to stop kidding myself. It took just a moment for me to make the decision to **"Admit it"**, and repent of my sin, but it took process and time to **"Quit it"**; showing proof I had completely changed my sin nature or ways. Likewise, I **"Believed"** immediately in my spirit, but **"Receiving"**, took time as I went through the process. Going through process and time strengthened my faith and refined my works. I had to fully submit to the Holy Spirit, so that the refiner's fire could produce a manifestation of God's work in my life.

The Word said, the manifestation would be according to the level of my faith. **Matthew 9:29** [Jesus is speaking]... According to your faith be it unto you. **Mark 11:24** [Jesus is speaking]...Therefore I say unto you, What things so ever ye desire, when ye pray, believe that ye receive them, and ye shall have them.

The present evidence showed I was receiving less than a thirty fold return on my efforts to affect change in my life and marriage. My marriage was sick; it was dying; and my marriage died right in front of me. I felt powerless to slow or prevent the downward spiral. I had come to a point in my relationship with the Lord that I needed an hundred fold return on His promises. I knew then I needed God's help to make my ways plain, and make my crooked ways straight.

My Crooked Way

In 1990, I divorced my first husband. For three years I lived with my son, as a single parent. By 1993, I believed that I was ready to start sharing my life with someone new. I began asking God to send someone to share the rest of my life with. The man who came was wonderfully made. **Side Note**: at that time in my life, I did not have a relationship with the Father. I was not called[2] by His name. I had not yet accepted Jesus Christ as my Lord and Savior. Yes God loved me, and yes, He cared for me. But I was outside of covenant with Him. God was not under any obligation to answer my prayers.

For two years I "low rated" myself" just so that me and this man could live together. I compromised on the values and beliefs my mother and father had taught me. I ignored the tug on my heart to come out of sin and seek a relationship with the Lord. After we had lived together for two years, I asked my boyfriend if our relationship was going to go beyond our present arrangement. He said, "No, I am not ready to be married".

At first, I was hurt then I became angry. I had been rejected. In truth, it was not his fault. Why? He was getting the milk for free, now suddenly I was trying to impose a "Usage Tax".

> **Wisdom Principle**: Any time you **low rate** yourself, and you try to raise the price you will lose your customer. I knew this principle. I even practiced it on occasion. "If I can get it for free, why should I pay for it?"

I had been rejected, so I struck back with *equal* vengeance. I asked him to move out, and he did. We were separated for a while. Six months later we did get married. But the foundation we built our marriage on was like the sand in the top half of an hour glass. It took nine years for all of the sand in our hour glass to run out.

For a short time the romance of courting in our sin relationship was pleasurable. When the honeymoon period was over, we settled into the routine of married life. But were we really married to each other? Before I answer this question, take this quick self examination.

Before you and your spouse were married:

○ Did the two of you discuss your core values and beliefs[3] concerning personal issues (i.e. communication, careers, personal space or personal mail)?

○ Did the two of you discuss your core values and beliefs on adultery, fornication, pornography, or any form of sexual sins?

○ Did the two of you discuss your core values and beliefs concerning social issues (i.e. alcohol or drug use, guns or weapons in the home, temper/physical violence, or profanity)?

○ Did the two of you decide to combine all assets and liabilities into one joint account?

○ Did the two of you discuss how and who would be responsible for paying the bills, and income taxes?

○ Did the two of you decide if or how many children you would have?

○ Did the two of you decide how the children would be raised?

○ Did the two of you decide on the division of domestic chores?

○ Did the two of you decide on whether or not you would attend church and practice your faith or type of religion?

If you are married, and the answers to any of these questions was no, you may be assuming too much of the other person. If these core values and belief questions were not shared, asked, or answered prior to marriage, your relationship with your spouse may be at risk. Your relationship is at risk of assuming too much anytime you come into contact with another person who was raised by parents other than yours.

Well for that matter even if they were raised by the same parents. **Case and point:** I have three sisters and one brother, and we were all raised in one household by our parents. Each of us has our own individual personality. But our life experiences have produced five very different adults. As siblings, we may share the same core values and beliefs our parents taught us, but by evidence in our expressed character traits, we each have produced some interesting exceptions to our parent's teachings.

Failing to communicate your core values and beliefs with your intended spouse prior to marriage is very risky business. You may be leaving them or yourself open for unintentional or intentional crossing of personal boundaries or personal space. Having unshared personal boundaries comes from the need to keep some things "private"; or "secret". Having secrets in a marriage is a form of division. **Amos 3:3** *Can two walk together except they be agreed?* But how can you agree on personal boundaries unless you share your boundaries openly before marriage?

And if by happenstance your spouse does cut across your unshared core values or beliefs concerning personal space or boundaries it could lead to hurt feelings, trust issues, bitterness, unforgiveness, all because of the now exposed need for privacy or secrecy. This crossing of personal boundaries may become that offense, or *"the last straw"* that steals, kills or destroys your covenant relationship. But there is another way. Let me show you the pattern.

God said He is "married" to us. **Jeremiah 3:14** The Lord is fully committed to us...forever. Being fully committed to our spouse in marriage is the pattern for how we should be living out our "married" lives. **Hosea 2:19 NLT** I will make you my wife forever, showing you righteousness and justice, unfailing love and compassion. **Genesis 2:24** says, "Therefore shall a man leave his father and his mother, and shall cleave unto his wife: and they shall be one flesh." You cannot be "one flesh" if you are single-minded living a married life.

Lesson Learned: Before entering into a covenant relation-ship, take time to know yourself and your true motives before committing to marriage. Notice that I did not say you should do this before committing to living in a sin relationship. Allow the full light of day to shine on the "real you". Know before you marry someone what are your "boundaries" and be willing to openly discuss them with your intended. If the "who you are" is not what they need, now is the time to look for another. But if you fail to do this self-check before marriage, you may find yourself asking questions like; "Why didn't I take the time to really get to know this person before I married them?" You may even make statements to yourself like; "If I knew this about them before I married them, I wouldn't have." You might even start thinking "I am not willing to help make this marriage work?" Or, you may take it even further, by asking your spouse for a separation or even a divorce.

But, now you have a big problem: you have knowledge, and you are married. If Jesus is your Lord, it is time to examine the field (your marriage) and the seeds (acknowledge your part) sown in it. Any seed, whether the seed was good or bad, you have sown in your marriage you will surely reap a harvest.

> **Matthew 13:24-30** Another parable put he forth unto them, saying, The kingdom of heaven is likened unto a man which sowed good seed in his field: But while men slept, his enemy came and sowed tares among the wheat, and went his way. But when the blade was sprung up, and brought forth fruit, then appeared the tares also. So the servants of the householder came and said unto him, Sir, didst not thou sow good seed in thy field? from whence then hath it tares? He said unto them, An enemy hath done this. The servants said unto him, Wilt thou then that we go and gather them up? But he said, Nay; lest while ye gather up the tares, ye root up also the wheat with them. Let both grow together until the harvest: and in the time of harvest I will say to the reapers, Gather ye together first the tares, and bind them in bundles to burn them: but gather the wheat into my barn.

Lesson Learned: Hindsight is always 20/20. From hindsight, I learned many powerful lessons. Unfortunately, I had to learn my lessons about how to be a good wife from the divorced state. I like to think, if I knew then what I know now, I would have done better by my husband and for myself.

When I looked back over my married life, and examined the seeds I sowed in the marriage the Holy Spirit helped me to see my mistakes, and He gave me, because I asked for wisdom, a vehicle to encourage others to choose to bypass the route to separation or divorce. This is why today I am so willing to be transparent in sharing with you my "woulda, coulda, shouldas". It is my hope you will choose not to come here.

I have been divorced more than six years now. And today, I can honestly say that I haven't found anything good about being divorced. First, I was 42 years old when I got divorced the second time. By the stroke of the judge's pen, my life suddenly started over. I felt as if I was beginning a new life. I felt as if I was 18 years old, leaving home for the first time. But...I had all these mental and physical memories of married life. At the stroke of a pen, I had to make all kinds of quick decisions. Where do I go? Where do I live? I was suddenly faced with two income debt, with a one income budget. I even had to come to terms with my new identity. Who am I?

When I was married taking care of my family's needs was important to me. Now dinner is usually chips and a soda. When I come home, I usually do not hear my voice again until I go back to work or when I go to church. If I am sick, the world doesn't stop. As sick as I may be, I must manage the strength to get to a doctor, or the store for medicine or food. Friends; yes, I have friends and coworkers, but they have their families too, and I am not one to bother others unless it is important or I need urgent assistance. Yes, I have the necessary things to be comfortable in life, but I agree with God, *"It is not good for man to be alone."*
Genesis 2:18

I believe I now have a better understanding of what things are good and important to sustain a healthy marriage and what things are detrimental to the covenant relationship. But for a moment, let us go back and examine the two central questions from *Psst! Are you Divorced? Are You Thinking About It*?

Chapter 2

Are You Divorced?

The bible says, "Nothing is impossible for God". The very next time, you hear this phrase, do yourself a favor; don't ask your best friend; don't even ask your family what did God mean by that statement? Ask the Lord for yourself.

Ask Him. Say, "Father, is the divorced state impossible for you to heal?" I believe that the Holy Spirit will tell you what he told me, "No. God is not a man that He should lie." **Numbers 23:19** The Holy Spirit will tell you, "Nothing is impossible for the Lord". **Luke 1:37** The Holy Spirit will exhort you to be of good courage. **Psalm 27:14** He will ask you to only believe. **Luke 8:50** The Holy Spirit will even ask you to prove God, and see if the Lord will not withhold anything good from you. **Malachi 3:10 and Psalm 84:11**

Well guess what? Divorce is something! If divorce is something, and it is, God wants to do something about it. **Hosea 4:6** "My people are destroyed for lack of knowledge: [and why?] because thou hast rejected knowledge,...." God wants to tell you something by way of the Holy Spirit. The Holy Spirit will tell you the truth the way God purposes for you to hear it. Divorce is a curse, and Jesus Christ, His son has redeemed you from the curse of divorce too.

I have witnesses for all the things I wrote about in my first book. You can check them out for yourself. In Chapter One of my first book I wrote how curses would come to destroy our future if my husband and I divorced. I knew then it would take fasting and prayer to hold back utter destruction. By September 2004, both of us suffered severe material losses, and yes, we were overwhelmed, but God kept us from being completely destroyed. In Chapter Two, I wrote a parable about a blue three eared rabbit, which is a metaphor for taking God at His word even when the word spoken seems to be foolishness. In July 2005, Blue Three-

Eared Rabbits® fully manifested in the earth. Then Chapter Seven speaks of the hope of restoration. In March 2006 the evidence of this hope pushed forth its first blade.

It did not take all three manifestations for me to praise the Lord. After each manifestation, I thanked God for His faithfulness! Why, because there are only eight chapters in the first book. And the Lord promised me an expected end. Now on to the second question; are you thinking about it...divorce I mean?

Chapter 3

Are You Thinking About It?

Have you heard this scripture? **Hebrews 11:1** "Now faith is the substance of things hoped for, the evidence of things not seen". Well, if you or your spouse is thinking about divorce, I pray you hear this next verse as well.

> **Galatians 5:19-21** (New King James Version, NKJV) Now the works of the flesh are evident, which are: adultery, fornication, uncleanness, lewdness, idolatry, sorcery, hatred, contentions, jealousies, outbursts of wrath, selfish ambitions, dissensions, heresies, envy, murders, drunkenness, revelries, and the like; of which I tell you beforehand, just as I also told *you* in time past, that those who practice such things will not inherit the kingdom of God.

Did you catch the similarity between the two verses? **"Now faith is...the evidence"**, and "**Now the works of the flesh are evident...,**" Both scriptures are speaking of a "right now" space in time.

It is also very interesting that in every single divorce you will find one, some or all of these works of the flesh, [or reasons], why husbands or wives think about divorce, or chose to get divorced. There are no exceptions to this rule. Test the rule out for yourself. Consider your own marriage, separation, divorce, or people whom you know well enough to know the reason for them to think about separation, divorce, or are now divorced, and you will find evidence that someone's flesh was at work, or their flesh is now working.

Said another way whenever the works of the flesh become evident divorce may happen. Remember, the works of the flesh can wreck your covenant relationship. If you or your spouse is thinking about divorce it is the "right now" time to discern what is really happening. Simply stated, the thief has come. And he has come on a specific assignment. The enemy has come to steal, kill, and to destroy your relationship with your spouse, with the ultimate goal of destroying your marriage. **John 10:10 NLT** The thief's purpose is to steal and kill and destroy.

> **To the Husband or Wife:** If the works of the flesh is on your part, will you continue to give the enemy place to rule and reign in your life? Or will you "admit it and quit it", turn and follow after Christ, and reconcile your relationship to your spouse?

> **To the Husband or Wife:** If the works of the flesh is on your spouse's part... you may have a stone in your hand, but are you free [of sin] yourself to throw the stone at them?

If either of these conditions fit your situation, it is the "right now" time to realize that the deceptions of the enemy are very deceitful. **Genesis 3:1** Now the serpent was more subtle than any beast.... **Why Principle**: "If it isn't broke don't fix or replace it." The enemy of old is still using the same tactics of deception to come between a husband and his wife.

After all these centuries, the enemy has just repackaged logic, intellect, reasoning, self will, personal desires, and personal weaknesses against a husband and his wife. For what reason? The enemy wants to defeat you in your covenant relationship. If you or your spouse takes the bait, you participate. But there is a way of escape. Forgive, and you shall be forgiven.

Chapter 4

The Narrow Gate Called Forgiveness

Now that you recognize Satan is trying to come between you and your spouse; reflect on this question. Is there any sin that you could commit that once you came to yourself, and you asked God to forgive you, He would turn His face from you? No, this is not a trick question, but there are two answers. The answers are: yes and no. I will explain.

> In **Matthew 12:31** it says, "all manner of sin and blasphemy shall be forgiven unto men, but blasphemy against the Holy Spirit will not be forgiven."

> In **Psalm 51:17** A broken and contrite heart, O God, thou wilt not despise.

Then what about your spouse? Is there any sin that your spouse can commit that once they come to themselves you feel you could not or will not forgive them for? Before you answer, let us consider the narrow gate called forgiveness. **Matthew 7:14 NKJV** Because narrow is the gate and difficult is the way which leads to life, and there are few who find it. God said, "forgive and you shall be forgiven." Right now you may not be there, but we must get to the point where we acknowledge that God said it, and we just "settle it", and forgive our spouse of all trespasses they may have committed against us.

> **Luke 6:37 NLT** If you forgive others, you will be forgiven.

> **Luke 11:4 NLT** Father...forgive us our sins – just as we forgive those how have sinned against us.

Luke 17:3 NLT If another believer sins, rebuke him; then if he repents, forgive him.

The number one reason why couples chose to divorce is because of sexual sin. But then what about **Jeremiah 3:1?** The Lord is speaking; *"If a man divorces a woman and she marries someone else, he is not to take her back again, for that would surely corrupt the land. But you have prostituted yourself with many lovers, says the Lord. Yet I am calling you to come back to me."*

Now you have to know that Jeremiah 3:1 pushed on me really hard because Jesus said in **Matthew 19:9 NLT**, "And I tell you this, a man who divorces his wife and marries another commits adultery – unless his wife has been unfaithful."

What do you do if your spouse has been unfaithful? For just a moment, forget about your spouse, and remember when you were once unfaithful to God. Remember when you were once lost to the kingdom of God. It is just you; standing in the need of salvation and prayer.

> **Colossians 1:21** And you, that were sometime alienated and enemies in your mind by wicked works, yet now hath he reconciled

> **Ephesians 2:12-13** That at that time ye were without Christ, being aliens from the commonwealth of Israel, and strangers from the covenants of promise, having no hope, and without God in the world: But now in Christ Jesus ye who sometimes were far off are made nigh by the blood of Christ.

> **Ephesians 4:17-19 (NLT)** With the Lord's authority I say this: Live no longer as the Gentiles do, for they are hopelessly confused. Their minds are full of darkness; they wander far from the life God gives because they have closed their minds and hardened their hearts against him. They have no sense of shame. They live for lustful pleasure and eagerly practice every kind of impurity.

Now consider your spouse, but before you do, you must first cover them, or wash them with the word as written in: **Romans 15:1,** *we then that are strong ought to bear the infirmities of the weak, and not to please ourselves.* You cover them when you forgive them. Now go, stand in the gap and pray for those who wander away from the truth.

> **Ezekiel 22:30 NLT** [God is speaking], I looked for someone who might rebuild the wall of righteousness that guards the land. I searched for someone to

stand in the gap in the wall so I wouldn't have to destroy the land, but I found no one.

Luke 23:34 Father, forgive them; for they know not what they do.

Acts 7:60 Lord, lay not this sin to their charge.

James 5:20 You can be sure that whoever brings the sinner back will save that person from death and bring about the forgiveness of many sins.

Through process and time, trial and error, I found out that *it is* easier to forgive when I chose of my own will to show and share the "God kind" of love. The "God kind" of love is unconditional and it covers a multitude of sins. **1 Peter 4:8 NLT**

1Corinthians 13:4 -7 NKJV Love suffers long and is kind; love does not envy; love does not parade itself, is not puffed up; does not behave rudely, does not seek its own, is not provoked, thinks no evil; does not rejoice in iniquity, but rejoices in the truth; bears all things, believes all things, hopes all things, endures all things. Love never fails.

Chapter 5

The Questions, and the Ready Answer

1Peter 3:15 But sanctify the Lord God in your hearts: and be ready always to give an answer to every man that asketh you a reason of the hope that is in you with meekness and fear:

Since releasing my book, *Psst! Are You Divorced? Are You Thinking About It?* there are five predominate questions people ask me to give them advice concerning their marriage, separation, or divorce:

1. Should I leave my spouse?

2. Should I have stayed in a sick, dying or dead marriage?

3. What if we are "two different" people going in opposite directions?

4. What if your spouse committed sexual sins?

5. When is enough; enough?

Whenever I am asked these questions, please forgive my hesitation if I don't answer you quickly or directly. The answers to your questions are so very personal. I now know that the decision to stay in a marriage or to end a marriage carries with it generational and eternal consequences.

Exodus 20:5 NLT …for I, the LORD your God, am a jealous God who will not tolerate your affection for any other gods. I lay the sins of the parents upon their children; the entire family is affected—even children in the third and fourth generations of those who reject me.

Malachi 2:14-16 AMP Yet you ask, Why does He reject it? Because the Lord was witness [to the covenant made at your marriage] between you and the wife of your youth, against whom you have dealt treacherously and to whom you were faithless. Yet she is your companion and the wife of your covenant [made by your marriage vows]. And did not God make [you and your wife] one [flesh]? Did not One make you and preserve your spirit alive? And why [did God make you two] one? Because He sought a godly offspring [from your union]. Therefore take heed to yourselves, and let no one deal treacherously and be faithless to the wife of his youth. For the Lord, the God of Israel, says: I hate divorce and marital separation and him who covers his garment [his wife] with violence. Therefore keep a watch upon your spirit [that it may be controlled by My Spirit], that you deal not treacherously and faithlessly [with your marriage mate].

A dear friend of mine would often say, "Well, all I know is…" then she would fill in what she knew God had said in His word, the Holy Bible. Using her template let me say, "Well all I know is", and then I will follow up by providing the bible reference that answers the question. I also encourage you to study out the Holy Scriptures for yourself. See first hand what is in God's word and what is on His heart concerning marriage, and divorce. When you study God's word, you will find out what are the husband's responsibilities to his wife; and what are the wife's responsibilities to her husband? What does God say to husbands and wives concerning the covenant relationship? What does God say about raising children and taking care of the home?

As for me: when I was confronted with a sick, dying, and then dead marriage; I read **1Corinthians 7:10** where it says, "Let not the wife leave her husband." I stayed in the marriage, and fulfilled my marital obligations until all hope faded.

When I was served with the petition for dissolution, I faced the decision whether to contest the divorce or not. In my spirit I heard, **1 Samuel 17:47** "…for the battle was the LORD's."
Having heard; I chose to not contest the divorce action. I believe for my obedience, I was given a measure of faith to walk into the court room believing that God was able to keep what I had committed to Him. Within three months after the divorce all of the old material things I had lost, were restored to me brand new.

When I was sent away, I was led to read **Jeremiah 29:14**: And I will be found of you, saith the LORD: and I will turn away your captivity, and I will gather you from all the nations, and from all the places whither I have driven you, saith the LORD; and I will bring you again into the place whence I caused you to be carried away captive." On this promise I continue to stand. I remind Him who promised me: "Father, you said…. Father, you caused my heart to believe". And as a watchman I will give Him no rest until He makes marriage a praise in the earth.

Yes, it has been several years since the divorce. Now after I have shared my testimony I am asked new questions and some have even given me counsel.

How long will you believe God? Well, all I know is…that I am fully persuaded that what He promised, He is able also to perform. **Romans 4:21** Whenever the length of time or the loneliness challenges my mind, or causes my heart to falter, I meditate on or rehearse those things the Holy Spirit has taught and revealed to me.

You say that you and your former spouse are very good friends; so what is the problem; why aren't you two back together again? All I know is… it is not the appointed time for me to marry. Until it is time for me to marry, I choose to live by my faith.

> **Habakkuk 2:3-4** For the vision is yet for an appointed time, but at the end it shall speak, and not lie: though it tarry, wait for it; because it will surely come, it will not tarry! The just shall live by his faith.

As for my former spouse, he has since reconciled his relationship with the Lord. God was faithful to perform His word when He reconciled him back into the kingdom.

A Note from my Journal
7 September 2004

This morning I woke up thinking about, **2 Corinthians 6:17** "Therefore come out from them and separate yourselves from them, says the Lord." So I asked, "Father how do I do this new thing, (*believe for the restoration of the first covenant relationship*), and for how long should I wait? Tell me how did Jesus sit down and wait until His enemies were made His footstool?" The answer that came to me was simple. Jesus had confidence, faith, and trust in the Father. The Holy Spirit brought me back to this scripture:

Matt 22:44 The LORD said unto my Lord, Sit thou on my right hand, till I make thine enemies thy footstool?

Now back to the question of how long must I wait for the restoration of the first covenant relationship? Well, I have decided to sit down and wait until the Lord makes my enemies my footstool. Why, because Jesus explained it best in **Mark 13:32** "But of that day and that hour knoweth no man, no, not the angels which are in heaven, neither the Son, but the Father."

To put this verse in Adriene's vernacular, "I just need to quit bugging Jesus. He doesn't know, else he would tell me. If I want to be more like Jesus, then I need to just sit, and put my confidence, faith, and trust in the Father! This battle is not mine, but the Lord's!"

Why did you keep your married name? All I know is…I am not ashamed of the gospel. In my first mind I originally planned on releasing my first book under my maiden name, Roberson. One night I woke up with the following statement on my mind: *"You are not ashamed of the gospel."* Not fully understanding the statement, I picked up my bible and was led to **Romans 1:16,** where it says: *"For I am not ashamed of the gospel of Christ: for it is the power of God unto salvation to every one that believeth;..."* For me this meant if I was to be a true witness for the Restoration of the First Covenant Relationship I could not turn my back on the family I was called to. To renounce the name "Dallas" was for me like being ashamed of the gospel truth.

Also when you take on a family name, you become a representative of that family. For me to live as the so called "sophisticated" lady would not bring honor to the Dallas family name. The name of Dallas reminds me of my purpose and my assignment. The name Dallas keeps me on the path to my destiny. The Dallas family name is my reminder of just whose I am.

Do I date? No, I do not date. A wife has no need to look for another. A wife has no need to date. I choose to live a virtuous and celibate life. **Proverbs 12:4 NLT** *A worthy wife is her husband's joy and crown; a shameful wife saps his strength.* Having said that, then came the greater challenge. I have to walk the talk. I purposefully take on this challenge, because I know that there is someone out there watching my life. Someone out there is depending on me to make it, so that they will know how to make it too. I know that there is someone out there who is waiting for someone like me, who is willing to be made a shame, and a spectacle. Even right now there is someone out there asking God to show them the way out. And if that someone is you, Jesus Christ is the way, the truth, and the life.

All I know is... the reports are coming back where husbands and wives are reconciling their relationships with the Lord and with each other. There are many testimonies about whole families turning back to Christ. Hearing these reports is like receiving good news. I am encouraged all the more to stand on the promise.

Yes, I have heard the questions and I have heard both positive and negative comments. There have been some well meaning individuals who have given advice that I even considered. Their words of wisdom seemed to be good enough of a reason to abandon the vision, and choose to go after my own life. Their wisdom seemed logical enough for me to choose to end the discomfort of being in a divorced state. But...I am not my own. My life is no longer mine. I was bought at a great price.

A Note from my Journal

Father, is it really up to me how long I will believe in your promises? Can I really tell you when I have had enough of this suffering? The answer came to me from, **Hebrews 11:6** *But without faith it is impossible to please him: for he that cometh to God must believe that he is, and that he is a rewarder of them that diligently seek him.*

I understand now why it is so vitally important for me to guard my heart. Now whenever I have questions, I take them to the only wise God. Why, it was the Lord who caused my eyes to even see his Word. It was by His Spirit I received inspiration and revelation to hear the word of the Lord. Only the Lord alone has the answers to eternal life. It is His wise counsel I choose to hear. It is only His voice I will follow after. Jesus Christ, He is the author and finisher of my faith. My answer to all who ask: God's grace is sufficient for me.

> **Hebrews 11:11** Through faith also Sarah herself received strength... because she judged him faithful who had promised.

And just like Sarah, I choose to believe God. I choose to believe God for the restoration of the first covenant relationship. I am going after the prize that has an eternal weight of glory. **2Corinthians 4:17**

Jesus said in **Matthews 19:11 NLT** "Not everyone can accept this statement, only those whom God helps."

A Note from my Journal
Father, I thank you for helping me.

God said, "love never fails". Personally, I needed to know more about this "God kind of love" that never fails. If God said it, then I had to learn how to purpose in my heart to settle that word in my heart. In **Deuteronomy 30:19** God said: "He has set before me life and death, blessing and cursing:".... I chose life. I am going after the good part.

Chapter 6

Choose the Good Part!

Psalm 41:5 Mine enemies speak evil of me, When shall he die, and his name perish?

Psalm 71:10 For mine enemies speak against me; and they that lay wait for my soul take counsel together,...

Isaiah 54:6 For the LORD hath called thee as a woman forsaken and grieved in spirit, and a wife of youth, when thou wast refused, saith thy God.

It has been several years since the divorce, and I know that people talk about me behind my back. I know that people are watching me. I know that they are speaking in whispers, saying, "See how the Lord has forsaken her". I know that people lay in wait, watching for me to fail, to quit, to run, and turn coward. I know that they even watch me to see if I will curse God and die. I know because I am not ignorant of my environment. Daily and in spite of what it looks like; I choose the good part. Daily and in spite of what it feels like, I choose the good part.

Luke 10:38-42 Now it came to pass, as they went, that he entered into a certain village: and a certain woman named Martha received him into her house. And she had a sister called Mary, which also sat at Jesus' feet, and heard his word. But Martha was cumbered about much serving, and came to him, and said, Lord, dost thou not care that my sister hath left me to serve alone? bid her therefore that she help me. And Jesus answered and said unto her, "My dear Martha, you are so upset over all these details! There is really only one thing worth being concerned about. Mary has discovered it – and I won't take it away from her."

This biblical account is about two sisters named Mary and Martha. The focus of the story is **"What Did Mary Do?"** When we focus on what Mary did, we learn we should like Mary position ourselves to hear the word of truth. We should position ourselves to be taught by the Holy Spirit. When we position ourselves to hear from the Lord, we learn we should not be pressed by the issues of life the way Martha was. When we sit at the Master's feet we learn how to focus on solutions for our relationships like Mary did, and not the problems the way Martha did.

After reading this story, I wondered; why did Mary sit at Jesus' feet? And just what did Mary hear while she was sitting at His feet? Before I answer these questions it is sufficient to say, Mary is our example for living. Mary is our pattern for how we should consider our own circumstance(s). We must focus first on our relationship with Christ. Building a relationship with the Lord makes for a solid foundation on which to build any other type of relationship. A marriage founded in Christ is *the* example your children should grow up watching and emulating.

In **Matthew 6:33**, it says: *"But seek ye first the kingdom of God, and his righteousness; and all these things shall be added unto you."* Once we have received instruction from the Holy Spirit, we should examine the issues of our own life. What upsets you? What man made details distract you or preoccupies your time, so much so that the distraction steals precious time away from you having a full relationship with the Lord, your spouse, or your family? A self examination will show you areas where you are falling short of receiving the promises of God or the rich fulfillment in marriage. Let us take a quick look at the Prophet Elijah.

1 Kings 19:11-13 NKJV Then He said, "Go out, and stand on the mountain before the LORD." And behold, the LORD passed by, and a great and strong wind tore into the mountains and broke the rocks in pieces before the LORD, *but* the LORD *was* not in the wind; and after the wind an earthquake, *but* the LORD *was* not in the earthquake; and after the earthquake a fire, *but* the LORD *was* not in the fire; and after the fire a still small voice. So it was, when Elijah heard *it,* that he wrapped his face in his mantle and went out and stood in the entrance of the cave. Suddenly a voice *came* to him, and said, "What are you doing here, Elijah?"

In this story we see that Elijah, the prophet, was dealing with an issue: Jezebel the queen wanted him dead. When Elijah heard her edict, he ran and hid in a cave, but the Lord was not in the issues (the wind, the earthquake, or the fire). God was in the solution. He even called to Elijah in a still small voice to come out of the cave, but Elijah did not come when first called. God allowed Elijah time to process all of the issues. When Elijah finally came face to face with in and of himself he did not have the answers to save his life, he heard the still small voice, and came out of the cave because God had his answer.

If you are having challenges with the issues in your life, then it is time to come and sit at the Master's feet and be taught of Him. Choose the good part. Prior to coming to sit before the Lord, prepare your heart and mind for an encounter with Him. Position yourself to hear directly from the throne. And when you come before the Lord, you must come to the throne of grace blameless. Do not hinder your prayers by allowing any unrepentance, bitterness, or unforgiveness to linger in your heart. Also, when you come to sit before the Lord, enter into His presence by way of praise and worship. If you are in need of God's assistance, it is at the throne where you can obtain mercy to help you in your time of need.

I too have discovered that there is *"only one thing worth being concerned about;"....* So the next time you see me and it

46

looks like I have not obtained what God has promised me; know that I am still there. I am still sitting at the throne of grace being taught by the Holy Spirit. Jesus promised that if I seek first the kingdom of God – *"the good part"*; if I choose His way of righteousness, and His way of doing, He won't take it away from me."

I am going after the good part!

Chapter 7

If God Said It, Settle It!

I believe that God has such a desire for His people, the body of Christ, and specifically husbands and wives, to hear, to receive and to walk according to His will and purposes. I know first hand how difficult it is to believe for the restoration of the first covenant relationship. I know because I found hearing the revelation hard to conceive. After I heard the word, I found it was hard to believe, and even harder to walk the talk. The bible says **it** [*the restoration of the first covenant relationship*] is impossible for man, but **with God** all things are possible. **Mark 10:27** I have tried the world's way of reconciliation and failed miserably. This time I am going with God.

But I had a problem. I did not have anyone to instruct me in the things I was being shown. When I asked God for help, the Holy Spirit led me to,

> **Hebrews 5:12** For when for the time ye ought to be teachers, ye have need that one teach you again which be the first principles of the oracles of God; and are become such as have need of milk, and not of strong meat.

Did you know that the divorce rate in the body of Christ is just as high as the divorce rate is in the secular world? Among married born again Christians, 35 percent have experienced a divorce. That figure is identical to the outcome among married adults who are not born again.[4] Why is that? I find it difficult to understand, because we, the body of Christ, we have God's own word that, "Nothing is impossible for Him." So what is keeping us, the body of Christ from believing God concerning our covenant relationship? God calls divorce a curse. We, the body of Christ know that God sent His only begotten son, Jesus Christ to redeem us from the curse. So again I ask, what is keeping us, the body of Christ from believing God concerning the restoration of the first covenant relationship?

I found out what is the source for the hardness of our (the body of Christ) hearts towards God's word. Satan is keeping us blinded to the truth by his deceptions. My husband and I took the bait, and we participated in the destruction of our covenant relationship. We went after our own liberties, and our own understanding of what was truth or right.

Now that I know the truth, I have become just like the woman who pleaded with the "unjust" judge, until he answered her. **Luke 18:1-8** The day my marriage died, I brought my complaint to the Lord. I said, "Father my marriage is dead." He said, "I can make dry bones live". Jesus said, "I have overcome death". And the Holy Spirit exhorted me to just believe. Today you can find me kneeling at the mercy seat pleading before a Just King. "Father, I will not give you rest until you make marriage a praise in the earth."

> **Luke 18:7 NLT** Even he [the unjust judge] rendered a just decision in the end, so don't you think God will surely give justice to his chosen people who plead with him day and night?

Have you heard these two clichés: "What Would Jesus Do (WWJD)?" and "God said It; Settle It"? Yes, these clichés are widely known, but have you ever actually taken the time to search out the bible to find out what did Jesus actually do? And what did God really say?

Here is a quick test: If God whispered in your ear right now: **"Psst! There are blue three eared rabbits at your feet".** Would you believe God, and look down, expecting to see blue three eared rabbits? The bible tells us in **Psalms 119:89** For ever, O LORD, thy word is settled in heaven. Then if God said it, settle it. Look…blue three eared rabbits!

Okay, when I first heard the question, I laughed too. I did not pass the "God said it; Settle it" test either. The very idea of blue three eared rabbits was too unbelievable. But God is known for taking the foolish things to confound the wise.

> **1 Corinthians 1:27** But God hath chosen the foolish things of the world to confound the wise; and God hath chosen the weak things of the world to confound the things which are mighty.

In that moment of clarity I saw what Jesus saw; the harvest **is** plenty, but the laborers are few. **Matthew 9:36-38** But when he [Jesus] saw the multitudes, he was moved with compassion on them, because they fainted, and were scattered abroad, as sheep having no shepherd. Then saith he unto his disciples, the harvest is plenteous but the labourers are few; Pray ye therefore he Lord of the harvest that he will send forth labourers into his harvest.

We the body of Christ, we have God's word, *why are* we still choosing to divorce our spouses as if we had never heard, or even tasted the word of God? We the body of Christ, are sadly choosing our own will over the will of God. It was then that I decided I wanted to learn what was written in the Holy Bible about the first covenant relationship and divorce.

I know the hurt and ache that comes from losing a spouse to divorce. I know about the disorientation that comes to your mind when the loss of a spouse causes confusion in every area of your life. I know about anguish so great that you feel as if your heart is being ripped to shreds. I know the sorrow a soul feels when your life is torn asunder. I know because divorce is a curse. And a curse is torment. Being tormented is like being in hell. To me being divorced is a type of hell.

And yet, we, the body of Christ were redeemed from the curse of divorce too! When Jesus died on Calvary's cross, he tore down the enemy's veil of deception. The enemy's tricks and lies were spoiled. The lie of divorce has been exposed by God's truth. I have decided to take my place in His harvest. I am sharing all that I have been taught, and I am telling all that I have seen. May God receive all the glory as heaven's population increases.

Romans 10:14 How then shall they call on him in whom they have not believed? and how shall they believe in him of whom they have not heard? and how shall they hear without a preacher?

A Note from my Journal

Father, I am willing to go teach deliverance to those blinded to the truth. I am willing to go tell those who are being held captive by the lies and tricks of the enemy. I am even willing to go speak encouragement to the brokenhearted, and give comfort to them that are bruised. If you send me, I will go tell them that salvation has come this hour to their house. Father, as your Holy Spirit leads me I will speak. Lord, send me.

I was twice married and now twice divorced. This testimony simply means I have experienced being both married and divorced. Though I have some experience with marriage and divorce, I do not know all the answers for everybody or for everyone's situation. But I know that the Lord, our God has your answer. If you dare to trust Him, and you have a desire to be a better husband or a better wife, you will find Heaven's Response® to any situation, circumstance, problem, or challenge that you might be having in your marriage written in the Holy Bible. All I know to do is encourage you to settle **Joshua 1:8** in your heart.

Joshua 1:8 This book of the law [the Holy Bible[5]] shall not depart out of thy mouth; but thou shalt meditate therein day and night, that thou mayest observe to do according to all that is written therein; for then thou shalt have good success.

In the next three chapters, you will find scriptures to meditate on just for husbands, scriptures just for wives; and scriptures that speak corporately to a husband and his wife. There are even scriptures that speak to children of divorce. God is so good! The references are not an all inclusive list. It is my hope to give you a place to start the process of reading some of what is in God's word until you come to the point of desiring to seek more of Him for yourself. I have learned that once I began to seek more of Him, I was able to settle more and more of His word in my heart. As I practiced His principles in my life, soon came the evidence I was in fellowship with the Lord. Faith came by hearing. And my hearing came as I consistently meditated on the word of God. **Romans 10:17**

Once the Word is settled in your heart, you can start applying what you heard and learned in your life. Expect God to move in and through your life, situations and circumstances. Go ahead place a demand on the Lord. If you abide in Him, and He abides in you, there is nothing you can not ask Him. When you make your requests known to Him, and ask according to His will, He will not withhold any good thing from you.

> **John 15:7** If ye abide in me, and my words abide in you, ye shall ask what ye will, and it shall be done unto you.

> **1 John 5:14** This is the confidence that we have in him, that if we ask any thing according to his will, he hearth us. And if we know that he hear us, whatsoever we ask, we know that we have the petitions that we desired of him.

> **Psalm 84:11** …no good thing will he withhold from them that walk uprightly.

Chapter 8

"All I Know"...For Husbands

There is one thing predictable about human nature; whenever there is a problem the first instinct is to deflect the problem or attention from you to projecting it onto someone else. But God is not fooled. He knows your heart, and He even knows your thoughts. **Psalm 94:11, Psalm 139:23** There is none good, no not one. **Romans 3:12**

Husbands, if it seems like you are the only one who recognizes that there are problems in your marriage; guess what? You are the one the Lord is trying to speak to. Husbands, as the head of the household, if order is going to be reestablished in your home, order should first come to the head of the household.

> **Question:** Is it biblically correct to say that the husband is the head of the household"? Yes.

> **1Timothy 3:2** specifically says a bishop is the husband of one wife. Women are never referred to in the Holy Scriptures as husband. A son yes; A husband not once. **1Timothy 3:5** goes on to say "(For if a man know not how to rule his own house, how shall he take care of the church of God?)" In order for the husband to be in the position to rule (lead) his own house he has to be in the position as the head of the household.

> In the time of the writing of the New Testament bishops were males. The present day church may have become lenient in doctrine by allowing females to become bishops. Am I willing to go far enough to say that the church is out of order? No. I am content to leave this debate up to **Ephesians 4:3**

Till we all come in the unity of the faith, and of the knowledge of the Son of God, unto a perfect man, unto the measure of the stature of the fulness of Christ:... Said another way; I am *resolved not to dispute over doubtful things*.... **Romans 14:1-12**.

In **Luke 1:17** "And he will go on before the Lord, in the spirit and power of Elijah, to turn the hearts of the fathers to their children and the disobedient to the wisdom of the righteous—to make ready a people prepared for the Lord." Looking at **Luke 1:17** with **Amos 3:3** subordinate to it, I wondered why the wife was not mentioned in Luke 1:17. I believe that it is because it is God's order that the father is to be the head (ruler) of the household, and that the wife is to be in subjection to her husband. So than how can two walk together, except they be agreed [in the raising of the children]? **Following the like as principle - John 14:7, and 9**...If you have seen the Son, you have seen the Father. [If you have seen the wife you have seen also the husband, why, because they are one flesh.]

Question: Well then what happens if the husband, whether it be because of death or divorce is not in the position as the head of the household? God, Himself answers this question in Isaiah 54:4-6.

Isaiah 54:4-6 Fear not; for thou shalt not be ashamed: neither be thou confounded; for thou shalt not be put to shame: for thou shalt forget the shame of thy youth, and shalt not remember the reproach of thy widowhood any more. For thy Maker is thine husband; the LORD of hosts is his name; and thy Redeemer the Holy One of Israel; The God of the whole earth shall he be called. For the LORD hath called thee as a woman forsaken and grieved in spirit, and a wife of youth, when thou wast refused, saith thy God.

Our Father is a God of order. If there is going to be any change in your covenant relationship, the Lord will call to the husband first. **Genesis 3:9** The Lord God called to Adam, "Where are you?" Husbands, harden not your heart. Come back to the Lord, and He will teach you how to draw your spouse with loving kindness. But first things first.

Husbands, the Lord is calling to you to come before Him. In **Isaiah 43:26 NLT,** [the Lord speaking] Let us review the situation [your part in the covenant relationship] together, and you can present your case if you have one.

> **2 Corinthians 13:5 NLT** Examine yourselves to see if your faith is really genuine. Test yourselves. If you cannot tell that Jesus Christ is among you, it means you have failed the test.

> **Psalm 26:2 NLT** Put me on trial, Lord, and cross-examine me. Test my motives and affections.

For me personally, I found I was able to hear and speak to God, whenever I got away from earthly distractions. Moses, David, and even Jesus went to a quiet place to be with the Lord. I found, when you get before the Lord, and allow the Holy Spirit to help you to examine yourself, the Holy Spirit *will* show you, you. If need be, after you have repented for your sins or iniquities, it is time to start declaring exactly what God has said; to settling His word in your heart. Rehearse these scriptures. Bring each one back to the Lord's remembrance. And don't let Him go until He, the one who promised, blesses you.

> **Jeremiah 6:5** Then said I, Woe is me! for I am undone; because I am a man of unclean lips, and I

dwell in the midst of a people of unclean lips: for mine eyes have seen the King, the LORD of hosts.

2 Samuel 12:13 And David said unto Nathan, I have sinned against the LORD.

1 John 3:19-22 And hereby we know that we are of the truth, and shall assure our hearts before him. For if our heart condemn us, God is greater than our heart, and knoweth all things. Beloved, if our heart condemn us not, then have we confidence toward God. And whatsoever we ask, we receive of him, because we keep his commandments, and do those things that are pleasing in his sight.

Joshua 1:8,9 NLT Study this Book of the Law continually. Meditate on it day and night so you may be sure to obey all that is written in it. Only then will you succeed. I command you - be strong and courageous! Do not be afraid or discouraged. For the Lord your God is with you wherever you go.

In this next segment, you will find two major verses with three supporting verses. The major verses are what God said. The supporting verses will help you to settle and apply the word in your life, before your wife, and your family. Anytime you are challenged with the supporting verse go back to the major verse to hear again what God said, then practice settling the word in your heart until you can show proof that the word is in your life. The proof that the word has manifested in your life will be by way of your works. The proof will be the evidence that the word has transformed your heart and mind into the mind of Christ.

Major verse: 1 Corinthians 13:7,8 NLT Love never gives up, never loses faith, is always hopeful, and endures through every circumstance. Love never fails....

Supporting verse: Acts 16:31 And they said, Believe on the Lord Jesus Christ, and thou shalt be saved, and thy house[6].

Supporting verse: Ephesians 5:25-28 (NLT) And you husbands must love your wives the same love Christ showed the church. He gave up his life for her to make her holy and clean, washed by baptism and God's word. He did this to present her to himself as a glorious church without a spot or wrinkle or any other blemish. Instead, she will be holy and without fault. In the same way, husbands ought to love their wives as they love their own bodies. For a man is actually loving himself when he loves his wife.

Supporting verse: 1 Peter 3:7 Likewise, ye husbands, dwell with them according to knowledge, giving honour unto the wife, as unto the weaker vessel, and as being heirs together of the grace of life; that your prayers be not hindered.

Major verse: Colossians 3:19 Husbands, love your wives, and be not bitter against them.

Supporting verse: James 5:16 The prayers of a righteous man availeth much.

Supporting verse: Matthew 5:44 But I say unto you, Love your enemies, bless them that curse you, do good to them that hate you, and pray for them which despitefully use you, and persecute you;

Supporting verse: Ephesians 6:12-14 12 For we do not wrestle against flesh and blood, but against principalities, against powers, against the rulers of the darkness of this age, against spiritual *hosts* of wickedness in the heavenly *places*. 13 Therefore take up the whole armor of God, that you may be able to withstand in the evil day, and having done all, to stand. 14 Stand therefore, having girded your waist with truth, having put on the breastplate of righteousness,

Chapter 9

The Play Book

Tomorrow the "Underdog" team will go for the championship against the only team in the league that has not lost a single game the entire season. The undefeated team's offense is unstoppable. Their defense quickly captures the advantage, and scores. To watch the undefeated team is a knuckle biting experience. How does the undefeated team pull off all those spectacular plays? If you could, would you like to have just one hour to study the undefeated team's play book?

I hope I did not lose some of you in the transition from husbands to wives. If you are truly serious about seeing positive changes in your marriage, you can see the other team's play book. To do just that all you have to do is read the Holy Bible. This is beauty of God's design for the Holy Bible; there is no need for any secrets between a husband and his wife. God purposefully set it up just that way. Husbands can read the play book about the mystery of women, and the wives can read the play book about the mystery of men.

When the husband and wife read the play book an opportunity comes for their hearts to be turned back to the Lord. And if the husband and wife allow, the Holy Spirit will turn their hearts back to each other. When the husband and wife come back to the knowledge that they are one the rest of the family becomes victorious too.

> **Luke 1:17** And he shall go before him in the spirit
> and power of Elias, to turn the hearts of the fathers to
> the children, and the disobedient to the wisdom of the
> just; to make ready a people prepared for the Lord.

The Holy Bible is the play book for the victorious. The bible will show husbands and wives how to be more than conquerors in any situation, circumstance, or challenge that surfaces through out their covenant relationship. The bible has instructions that will teach husbands and wives how two can put ten thousand fleeing. **Deuteronomy 32:30** The bible is God's play book on how to pull down strong holds to the saving of souls. **James 5:19-20** The word of the God is able to teach both husbands and wives how they can and should live their lives together...in Christ.

> **1Pet 3:1-7** Wives, likewise, *be* submissive to your own husbands, that even if some do not obey the word, they, without a word, may be won by the conduct of their wives, when they observe your chaste conduct *accompanied* by fear. Do not let your adornment be *merely* outward—arranging the hair, wearing gold, or putting on *fine* apparel— rather *let it be* the hidden person of the heart, with the incorruptible *beauty* of a gentle and quiet spirit, which is very precious in the sight of God. For in this manner, in former times, the holy women who trusted in God also adorned themselves, being submissive to their own husbands, as Sarah obeyed Abraham, calling him lord, whose daughters you are if you do good and are not afraid with any terror.

> **Ephesians 5:21-23** Submitting yourselves one to another in the fear of God. Wives, submit unto your own husbands, as unto the Lord. For the husband is the head of the wife, even as Christ is the head of the church: and he is the saviour of the body.

If your covenant relationship is sick, dying or dead, I challenge you to study the play book. Ask the Holy Spirit to show you, you, and where you need change. After you have reviewed your team's play book, then study your spouse's play book. Try switching things up a bit. God says "Love never fails". Then be bold! Take God at his word and settle it. If your spouse is acting unlovable, practice sharing and showing God's kind of love towards them. Rekindle your interest in your spouse by esteeming their needs better than your own. **Philippians 2:3**. Show your spouse tenderness without demanding or expecting sexual intimacy. Seek to find out what, or if there are underlying issues blocking communication between you and your spouse.

By consistently applying by way of demonstration each new play until you have perfected it will work in every area of your entire relational life. The play book can also work in your family and friend relationships too. If your family or friend relationships do not look like what is described in the play book, change your ways, and esteem their needs better than your own.

People are more likely to change when they see you have changed. It is that age old adage "Your actions will speak louder than your words". When you study the play book, and consistently practice the play "love never fails", you will draw your family. Okay, your loved ones may be spectators right now, but sooner or later everyone wants to be on the winning team. Sooner or later they will want to get into the game with you. Trust God. Do what the Holy Spirit teaches you, and you too can draw your loved ones with loving kindness

Examples from the Play Book – For Men

Husbands and single men: The bible gives instructions to you on how to be a good husband, provider, and father. A good man is a man of honor, integrity, valor, vigilant, of good behavior, one who rules well his own house and children.

> **1 Timothy 3:2** A bishop then must be blameless, the husband of one wife, vigilant, sober, of good behaviour, given to hospitality, apt to teach;

> **1Peter 3:7** Likewise, ye husbands, dwell with them according to knowledge, giving honour unto the wife, as unto the weaker vessel, and as being heirs together of the grace of life; that your prayers be not hindered.

Titus 6 -9 NKJV If a man is blameless, the husband of one wife, having faithful children not accused of dissipation or insubordination. For a bishop must be blameless, as a steward of God, not self-willed, not quick-tempered, not given to wine, not violent, not greedy for money, but hospitable, a lover of what is good, sober-minded, just, holy, self-controlled, holding fast the faithful word as he has been taught, that he may be able, by sound doctrine, both to exhort and convict those who contradict.

Titus 2:2 Teach the older men to exercise self-control, to be worthy of respect, and to live wisely. They must have sound faith and be filled with love and patience. **6** In the same way, encourage the young men to live wisely.

Men: In the play book you will also find out how to recognize a virtuous woman. A virtuous woman or wife should have chaste conversation, having the ornament of a meek and quiet spirit, which is in the sight of God of great price. **1Peter 3:4** The husband can safely trust his wife. He will have no lack of gain. She does him good and not evil all the days of her life. **Proverbs 31:11**. Husbands, if the woman you have right now does not look like, or does not present herself as a virtuous woman; it is praying and declaring time.

Single men: If the woman you have does not look like nor acts like a virtuous woman it is time to look for another. Your chosen helpmeet should compliment you. **Genesis 2:18 AMP** Now the Lord God said, It is not good (sufficient, satisfactory) that the man should be alone; I will make him a helper meet (suitable, adapted, complementary) for him.

Examples from the Play Book – For Women

Wives and single women: You too can also look into the play book and find an example of a virtuous woman. **Read Proverbs 31:10-31**

To young single women, unmarried women, or widows if the desire of your heart is to be married then you should read **Titus 2:3-5**. This reference gives instructions on what it takes to be successful in marriage.

> **Titus 2:3-5 NLT** Similarly, teach the older women to live in a way that honors God. They must not slander others or be heavy drinkers. Instead, they should teach others what is good. These older women must train the younger women to love their husbands and their children, to live wisely and be pure, to work in their homes, to do good, and to be submissive to their husbands. Then they will not bring shame on the word of God.

Wives: If the man you have does not look like or does not act like a man who is after God's own heart or a man God would not fellowship with, it is praying and declaring time for you as well.

Single women: If the man you have does not look like or does not act like a man who is after God's own heart, or a man even God would not fellowship with...look for another. I do not recommend that you test your brakes...I mean faith to change your husband after you get married. **Lesson Learned**: You cannot change people. The only one you can effect change on is you. Take this avenue, and you are *in the express lane* to a crooked way.

Studying the play book will also help you to know what you did not know about yourself. The bible gives instructions to help you develop good interpersonal habits. The bible will help you to discern whether or not a relationship is good or one to avoid. Studying the play book will help you build up your prayer life and faith so you can do what you currently think you could not possibly do. The play book will teach you how to declare those things that be not as though they were [fully manifested]. **Isaiah 46:10**

Chapter 10

"All I Know"...For Wives

If the husband fails to respond to God's call to return to his headship in the covenant relationship, the Lord will then call to the wife.

> **Jeremiah 31:22 AMP** How long will you waver and hesitate [to return], O you backsliding daughter? For the Lord has created a new thing in the land [of Israel (the body of Christ)]; a female shall compass (woo, win, and protect) a man.

> **Exodus 4:25** [Apparently he (Moses) had failed to circumcise one of his sons, his wife being opposed to it; but seeing his life in danger] Zipporah took a flint knife and cut off the foreskin of her son and cast it to touch [Moses'] feet, and said, Surely a husband of blood you are to me!

> **1 Samuel 25:14, 24** Now one of the young men took Abigail, Nabal's wife, saying, "Look, David sent messengers from the wilderness to greet our master; and he reviled them. So she [Abigail] fell at his [David's] feet and said: "on me, my lord, on me let this iniquity be!"

And likewise to the wives, the Lord is saying, **Isaiah 43:26 NLT** Let us review the situation [your part in the covenant relationship] together, and you can present your case if you have one.

> **Psalm 26:2 NLT** Put me on trial, Lord, and cross-examine me. Test my motives and affections.

2 Corinthians 13:5 NLT Examine yourselves to see if your faith is really genuine. Test yourselves. If you cannot tell that Jesus Christ is among you, it means you have failed the test.

In the next segment, you will find a major verse and six supporting verses. The major verse is what God said. The supporting verses will help you to apply the word, or settle it. Anytime you are challenged with the supporting verse go back to the major verse to hear again what God has said, then work on settling the word in your heart. When the word is settled in your heart, prove that the word is in your life by faithfully demonstrating it before your husband and family.

Major Verse: 1 Corinthians 13:7 Love never gives up, never loses faith, is always hopeful, and endures through every circumstance.

> **Supporting Verse: Acts 16:31** And they said, Believe on the Lord Jesus Christ, and thou shalt be saved, and thy house.

> **Supporting Verse: Colossians 3:18** Wives, submit yourselves unto your own husbands, as it is fit in the Lord.

> **Supporting Verse: 1 Peter 3:1** Likewise, ye wives, be in subjection to your own husbands; that, if any obey not the word, they also may without the word be won by the conversation of the wives;

> **Supporting Verse: Matthew 5:44** But I say unto you, Love your enemies, bless them that curse you, do good to them that hate you, and pray for them which despitefully use you, and persecute you;

Supporting Verse: Ephesians 6:12-14 For we do not wrestle against flesh and blood, but against principalities, against powers, against the rulers of the darkness of this age, against spiritual *hosts* of wickedness in the heavenly *places*. Therefore take up the whole armor of God, that you may be able to withstand in the evil day, and having done all, to stand. Stand therefore, having girded your waist with truth, having put on the breastplate of righteousness,

Supporting Verse: James 5:16 The prayers of a righteous man availeth much.

A Note from my Journal
19 July 2002

Father, against you have I sinned. I now understand how my actions and my behavior hurt and worked to destroy my relationship with my husband. Lord, start me over. Give me a clean heart. Restore a right spirit in me. Break me and make me over into a virtuous help meet.

So What I Am Doing Until My Change Comes?

Luke 19:12-13 He said therefore, A certain nobleman went into a far country to receive for himself a kingdom, and to return. And he called his ten servants, and delivered them ten pounds, and said unto them, **Occupy till I come.**

A Note from my Journal

Father, I will occupy until your return. Holy Spirit, help me to be all about the Father's business.

Immediately, I heard in my spirit, "Meditate on **Proverbs 31:10-31** *This book of the law shall not depart out of thy mouth; but thou shalt meditate therein day and night, that thou mayest observe to do according to all that is written therein; for then thou shalt have good success.*"

> **A note to bible scholars:** I know that the above text is the text to **Joshua 1:8 KJV**, but the Holy Spirit instructed me to meditate on Proverbs 31:10-31, observe and obey everything written in it; then would I prosper and have good success.

The Virtuous Wife

Proverbs 31:10-12 Who can find a virtuous wife? For her worth is far above rubies. The heart of her husband safely trusts her; So he will have no lack of gain. She does him good and not evil All the days of her life.

A Note from my Journal
October 2004

Father, today was a good day. I received a phone call from "D", he asked me if I would watch his house while he was out of town. Wow, when he handed over to me the keys to his house, all I could do was look down at them. What it meant to me to receive the keys to his house even after our divorce was he trusts me with all that he has. Father, I thank you for blessing me to see this day.

What To Do Until The Promise Comes

Proverbs 31:13-22, 24-27: She seeks wool and flax, And willingly works with her hands. She is like the merchant ships, She brings her food from afar. She also rises while it is yet night, And provides food for her household, And a portion for her maidservants. She considers a field and buys it; From her profits she plants a vineyard. She girds herself with strength, And strengthens her arms. She perceives that her merchandise *is* good, And her lamp does not go out by night. She stretches out her hands to the distaff, And her hand holds the spindle. She extends her hand to the poor, Yes, she reaches out her hands to the needy. She is not afraid of snow for her household, For all her household *is* clothed with scarlet. She makes tapestry for herself; Her clothing *is* fine linen and purple. She makes linen garments and sells *them* And supplies sashes for the merchants. Strength and honor *are* her clothing; She shall rejoice in time to come. She opens her mouth with wisdom, And on her tongue *is* the law of kindness. She watches over the ways of her household, And does not eat the bread of idleness.

Post Script
September 2008

At this present time I am an unmarried woman. I care only for the things of the Lord. I purposefully keep myself holy both in body and in spirit. I continue to work on my professional career. Since the divorce the Lord has promoted me three times. The Lord has also blessed me to be able to establish three faith based businesses.

Until I am called home to be with the Lord, I will continue to work in His vineyard. The vineyard is called "the ministry of reconciliation". I will tell all of the Lord's faithfulness. I will show of His goodness. If you have ears to hear, allow these words to be an encouragement to your heart, "The Lord is not a respecter of persons". What He is doing in and through my life, He is showing you, telling you, and calling to you to also believe for the restoration of your first covenant relationship.

All I know is everyday more and more mysteries into the first covenant relationship are being revealed, and lives are being changed. Husbands are returning to their wives. Wives are returning to their husbands. And the hearts of fathers are turning back to their children. Whole families are being reconciled back to Jesus Christ. Glory to His most holy name!

Proverbs 31:23 Her husband is known in the gates, When he sits among the elders of the land.

A Message from Kenneth Dallas
28 March 2006

From: Dallas, Kenneth O
Sent: Tuesday, March 28, 2006 9:04 AM
To: Dallas, Adriene R
Subject: Books to Purchase

Good Morning Dear, I pray that you are doing well and this will be a great week for you. I want to purchase a book/s that I can read to obtain a better understanding of the Bible from Genesis to Revelation.

"D"

From: Dallas, Adriene R
Sent: Tuesday, March 28, 2006 9:35 AM
To: Dallas, Kenneth O
Subject: Books to Purchase

Babe, what is on your heart?

From: Dallas, Kenneth O
Sent: Tuesday, March 28, 2006 10:16 AM
To: Dallas, Adriene R
Subject: Books to Purchase

I want to learn more about Christ. Understand and live my life in accordance with his teaching. I want to get closer and build a relationship with Christ and gain the knowledge of the Holy Spirit and my spiritual purpose for being here. To have and live a better Christian life, be a living witness for the Lord, and become worthy of receiving blessings that God continues to bestow upon me.

A Note from My Journal
28 March 2006

Father, you have done it! You have been faithful to perform your word. This day the first blade came up! Kenneth *was* drawn with loving kindness! Kenneth Dallas' name is known in heaven. His name is even known among the elders in his church. Father, I thank you for your faithfulness.

Proverbs 31:28 Her children arise up, and call her blessed; her husband also, and he praiseth her.

From Dead to Diamonds

In 1994, when my son was 13 years old, he told me that he hated me and he said that he wished that I was dead. He told me that he did not want to see me anymore. To settle the discord between us, I agreed to give primary custody of my son over to his father. For four years I honored my son's request and did not try to see or speak to him. In 1998, on my birthday I asked the Lord, if I could talk to my son, and the Lord released me to call him. I asked my son if he would come and share lunch with me, and he said yes. As a birthday present, my son gave me a diamond necklace with matching diamond earrings.

For four years I prayed for my son. I prayed that my son would be reconciled to Christ. I prayed that my son and I would be reconciled back to each other. In July 1999, my son received Jesus Christ as his Lord and savior. It took four year of praying for me to go from being dead to diamonds. The cost of our separation was very painful. The cost to pray for those who say they hate you was a humble heart. Watching my son as he accepted Jesus Christ as his Lord and Savior was the reward.

- I Prayed -

Father, I am an ambassador for Christ, as though God did beseech me: I pray in Christ's stead that my son be reconciled to you Lord. **2 Corinthians 5:20**

Father, you said, "If I be saved, my whole house shall be saved"[7]. **Acts 16:31**

A Note from Kenneth Dallas
1 January 2007

Hi Love,

I pray you had a blessed and wonderful Holiday. I know God will continue to bestow his blessing upon you and this will be a very blessed and successful year for you and Living Waters Christian Books. How are you love? Have a blessed day.

Love,

Kenneth O. Dallas

A Note from My Journal
1 January 2007

Father, look, "D" is speaking blessings into my life! Joy! Joy! Father, you are so faithful to watch over your word. Your works are so marvelous!

Post Script
September 2008

To my dear brothers and sisters in the Lord;

I have not yet obtained the promise, but I receive encouragement from your cards and letters. Many of you have written that you are living the promise. All I know is if we observe to do according to God's will and purpose for our lives, we shall receive all that He has promised.

All I know to do is ensure that my faith and my actions are working together. All I know to do is work the word. All I know is when I work the word, my faith will be made complete.

A Note from My Journal

Father, when I have finished my race, I pray that you are able to say this about me:

Proverbs 31:29-31 "Many daughters have done well, But you excel them all. Charm is deceitful and beauty is passing, But a woman who fears the LORD, she shall be praised. Give her of the fruit of her hands, And let her own works praise her in the gates."

Matthew 25:21 Well done, thou good and faithful servant:

Chapter 11

"All I Know"...For Husbands And Wives

Husbands and wives, the Lord wants to speak to you together. But first, let me share with you an account of when God brought three people before Him for a moment of public chastisement. Oh, not to worry; God loves those he chastises.

> **Numbers 12:1-4** And Miriam and Aaron spake against Moses because of the Ethiopian woman whom he had married: for he had married an Ethiopian woman. And they said, Hath the LORD indeed spoken only by Moses? hath he not spoken also by us? And the LORD heard it. (Now the man Moses was very meek, above all the men which were upon the face of the earth.) And the LORD spake suddenly unto Moses, and unto Aaron, and unto Miriam, Come out ye three unto the tabernacle of the congregation. And they three came out.

In this account we can see that there are three people; Moses, Aaron, and Miriam. Moses is described as being very meek. We also see from the text that Aaron and Miriam spoke against Moses. And the LORD heard it. When God heard Aaron and Miriam speak against Moses, he commanded the three, Moses, Aaron, and Miriam come out in front of the entire congregation (meaning - all of the people were watching). To bring this account into context with the *Restoration of the First Covenant Relationship*; Moses represents the Holy Spirit. Aaron and Miriam represent the husband and his wife.

In every single divorce, the husband, his wife, or both, (whether it be ignorance or with knowledge), spoke against the work of the Holy Spirit. Husbands and wives, whenever you lean to your own understanding, you are in effect speaking against the

Holy Spirit. Anytime our thinking, or our way of being right is elevated, or exalted above the knowledge of God's wisdom, you are speaking against the work of Holy Spirit. Husbands and wives, on the day you enter into the divorce court to plead your case before the judge, (a public forum where people can stand witness), you are about to testify to heaven and earth against the person of the Holy Spirit. If you have ears to hear, than hear:

> **Malachi 2:14-16 NKJV** Yet you say, "For what reason?" Because the LORD has been witness between you and the wife of your youth, with whom you have dealt treacherously; yet she is your companion and your wife by covenant. But did He not make *them* one, having a remnant of the Spirit? And why one? He seeks godly offspring. Therefore take heed to your spirit, and let none deal treacherously with the wife of his youth. For the LORD God of Israel says that He hates divorce, for it covers one's garment with violence," says the LORD of hosts. Therefore take heed to your spirit, that you do not deal treacherously."

> **Deuteronomy 30:19-20 NLT** Today I have given you the choice between life and death, between blessings and curses. Now I call on heaven and earth to witness the choice you make. Oh, that you would choose life, so that you and your descendants might live! You can make this choice by loving the LORD your God, obeying him, and committing yourself firmly to him. This is the key to your life. And if you love and obey the LORD, you will live long in the land the LORD swore to give your ancestors Abraham, Isaac, and Jacob."

Husbands and wives, instead choose to lay aside all malice, all deceit, all hypocrisy, all envy, and all evil speaking...if indeed you have tasted that the Lord is good and gracious, leave the court room still husband and wife.

Tell Jesus' disciples and Peter....

I absolutely love the Lord for His kindness towards me. In **Mark 16:1-7**, Mary Magdalene, and Mary the mother of James, and Salome, brought spices so that they could anoint the dead body of Jesus. When they arrived at the grave site the stone was rolled away, and a young man was sitting on the right side, clothed in a long white garment; and they were afraid. The young man told them to not be afraid. He said that Jesus was not there, that he had risen. And they were to go tell Jesus' disciples and Peter.

> **Mark 16:6,7** ...but the angel said, "Don't be alarmed. You are looking for Jesus of Nazareth, who was crucified. He isn't here! He is risen from the dead! Look, this is where they laid his body. **7** Now go and tell his disciples, including Peter,....

Wait a minute, wasn't Peter was one of Jesus' disciples? Yes, he was. Then why were the three women instructed to go tell Jesus disciples *and Peter*? Let us look at the prophesy Jesus spoke over Peter's life. Jesus asked his disciples "who do you say that I am." **Matthew 16:15** When Peter answered, "You are the Christ, the Son of the living God." Jesus replied that Peter could only have received that revelation from God. And based on that revelation, Jesus would build His church. **Matthew 16:18** (Jesus speaking) And I say also unto thee, That thou art Peter, and upon this rock I will build my church; and the gates of hell shall not prevail against it.

In **John 13:36-38**, Jesus predicts that Peter would three times deny knowing him. Later, when Jesus was taken as a prisoner, three times Peter did deny knowing Jesus. Peter's denial of Jesus put him at risk of losing his salvation and aborting his destiny. The women were sent to recover Peter.

Still not fully understanding what the Lord was revealing to me, I asked again. 'Holy Spirit, how does this story relate to the divorced now remarried?' I heard in my spirit this explanation; *"This is a matter of recovering the sight to the blind (the lost sheep of Israel). Recover those who are married and thinking about divorce by encouraging them to focus on the Word of Truth to the saving of their souls and their marraige. Comfort those who are now divorced by sharing with them, that even though they may have divorced, they have an opportunity to repent, and sin no more."*

John 5:14 Afterward Jesus findeth him in the temple, and said unto him, Behold, thou art made whole: sin no more, lest a worse thing come unto thee.

John 8:10,11 When Jesus had lifted up himself, and saw none but the woman, he said unto her, Woman, where are those thine accusers? hath no man condemned thee? She said, No man, Lord. And Jesus said unto her, Neither do I condemn thee: go, and sin no more.

Tell the Divorced; Now Remarried

Matthew 19:7-12 NLT 7 "Then why did Moses say in the law that a man could give his wife a written notice of divorce and send her away?" they asked. Jesus replied, "Moses permitted divorce only as a concession to your hard hearts, but it was not what God had originally intended. And I tell you this, whoever divorces his wife and marries someone else commits adultery—unless his wife has been unfaithful," Jesus' disciples then said to him, "If this is the case, it is better not to marry!" "Not everyone can accept this statement," *Jesus said. "Only those whom God helps*. Some are born as eunuchs, some have been made eunuchs by others, and some choose not to marry for the sake of the Kingdom of Heaven. *Let anyone accept this who can.*"8

In this passage, Jesus is talking about the "body of Christ's" heart. If you have accepted Jesus Christ as your Lord and Savior, then you are urged to not harden your heart against the truth. In the day you become frustrated with your husband or your wife, do not harden your heart against them. On that day allow the Holy Spirit to correct you for your response to a dispute between you and your spouse.

But what if you have divorced and you are now remarried? Jesus gives us an answer: Jesus said. "Not everyone can accept this statement," Jesus said. Only those whom God helps. **Matthew 19:11 NLT** The question becomes; do you want the Lord to help you? If so, there is therefore now no condemnation to them which are in Christ Jesus, who walk not after the flesh, but after the Spirit. **Romans 8:1** Here is a self examination.

Are you in Christ Jesus? If your answer is "No", salvation is available to everyone.[9]

> **Romans 10:9-13 NLT** If you confess with your mouth that Jesus is Lord and believe in your heart that God raised him from the dead, you will be saved. For it is by believing in your heart that you are made right with God, and it is by confessing with your mouth that you are saved. As the Scriptures tell us, "Anyone who trusts in him will never be disgraced." Jew and Gentile are the same in this respect. They have the same Lord, who gives generously to all who call on him. For "Everyone who calls on the name of the LORD will be saved."

Are you in Christ Jesus? If you answered "Yes"; **are you walking after the Spirit?** If your answer is "No", then review how to walk in the fruit of the Spirit.

> **Galatians 5:22-25** But the fruit of the Spirit is love, joy, peace, longsuffering, gentleness, goodness, faith, meekness, temperance: against such there is no law. And they that are Christ's have crucified the flesh with the affections and lusts. If we live in the Spirit, let us also walk in the Spirit.

If you answered, yes, and you want God to help you, you should read:

> **1Corinthians 7:27 NLT** If you have a wife, do not seek to end the [current] marriage. If you do not have a wife, do not seek to get married.

Now I see right here some might need a little more help.

> **1 Corinthians 7:9** But if they cannot contain, let them marry: for it is better to marry than to burn.

Responsibilities Of The Husband And Wife

If your marriage does not look like what God says a marriage should look like, then do according to: **Jeremiah 43:26** [The Lord is speaking], Put me in remembrance: let us plead together: declare thou, that thou mayest be justified. But first things must be first:

2 Corintians 5:13 Examine yourselves, whether ye be in the faith; prove your own selves. Know ye not your own selves, how that Jesus Christ is in you, except ye be reprobates?

Matthew 7:2-4 For with what judgment ye judge, ye shall be judged: and with what measure ye mete, it shall be measured to you again. And why beholdest thou the mote that is in thy brother's eye, but considerest not the beam that is in thine own eye? Or how wilt thou say to thy brother, Let me pull out the mote out of thine eye; and, behold, a beam is in thine own eye?

Husbands - Your Role and Responsibility in the First Covenant Relationship

Ephesians 5:23 For the husband is the head of the wife, even as Christ is the head of the church: and he is the saviour of the body.

1 Peter 3:7 Likewise, ye husbands, dwell with them according to knowledge, giving honour unto the wife, as unto the weaker vessel, and as being heirs together of the grace of life; that your prayers be not hindered.

1 Timothy 3:2 A bishop then must be blameless, the husband of one wife, vigilant, sober, of good behavior, given to hospitality, apt to teach;

Ephesians 5:33 Nevertheless let every one of you in particular so love his wife even as himself;

1 Timothy 3:12 Let the deacons be the husbands of one wife, ruling their children and their own houses well.

Wives - Your Role and Responsibility in the First Covenant Relationship

Genesis 3:18 ...and thy desire shall be to thy husband, and he shall rule over thee.

Ephesians 5:24 Therefore as the church is subject unto Christ, so let the wives be to their own husbands in every thing.

Ephesians 5:33 ...the wife see that she reverence her husband.

1 Peter 3:1-7 NKJV Wives, likewise, *be* submissive to your own husbands, that even if some do not obey the word, they, without a word, may be won by the conduct of their wives, when they observe your chaste conduct *accompanied* by fear. Do not let your adornment be *merely* outward—arranging the hair, wearing gold, or putting on *fine* apparel— rather *let it be* the hidden person of the heart, with the incorruptible *beauty* of a gentle and quiet spirit, which is very precious in the sight of God. For in this manner, in former times, the holy women who trusted in God also adorned themselves, being submissive to their own husbands, as Sarah obeyed Abraham, calling him lord, whose daughters you are if you do good and are not afraid with any terror.

Draw Your Spouse with Loving Kindness

1 Corinthians 7:2 Nevertheless, to avoid fornication, let every man have his own wife, and let every woman have her own husband.

1 Corinthians 7:3 Let the husband render unto the wife due benevolence: and likewise also the wife unto the husband.

1 Corinthians 7:4 The wife hath not power of her own body, but the husband: and likewise also the husband hath not power of his own body, but the wife.

I have to admit it. I used sex, or the lack of sex as a weapon against my husband. If he made me angry, I would cross my legs for however long I felt he should pay for the offense. And as I did to my husband, I received my like share of neglect in return. I also learned that if you continue practicing this behavior in your marriage...my experience - no good will ever came of it. My husband and I opened doors for the enemy to attack our relationship. We gave place and room for the enemy to steal, kill, and ultimately he did, with our participation, destroyed our marriage. This is only one example where we allowed hurt, bitterness, envy, strife, jealousy, or selfishness ambitions to enter in and break up our marriage.

> **A Maturing Point**: No one can ever make you do anything. My reaction to any given situation is my own reaction. My husband didn't make me mad. I was presented with an opportunity, and I took the bait (the offense). I choose to be angry. And out of my sinful nature, I returned in kind. I have since learned that I own the power to choose to act or not react to any stimulus.

If your marriage is going by this way, instead choose to confess your faults one to another. Choose to pray one for another, that your relationship will be healed. The effectual fervent prayer of a righteous man availeth much. **James 5:16**

Draw an Unbelieving Spouse with Loving Kindness

Have you ever heard that "God will not bless your mess"? Well, I did. Interesting enough, I found several examples in the bible where God did in fact "bless our mess".

> **Example:** Abraham and Sarah tried to help God, by having a child through Sarah's handmaid Hagar. God blessed Abraham's mess when he and Sarah stepped out before God's timing! Hagar gave birth to the child, Ishmael. Because Ishmael was Abraham's seed, God blessed Ishmael. God blessed Abraham's mess.

>> **Genesis 21:13** The angel of God called to Hagar saying, Genesis 21:19 "Arise, and lift up the lad, and hold him in thine hand; for I will make him a great nation."

> **Example:** David, seduced a married woman named, Bathsheba. David caused Bathsheba to become pregnant. Then David had Bathsheba's husband Uriah killed in battle. After the death of Uriah, David married Bathsheba. When David's sins were exposed; David cried before the Lord. **Psalm 51:17** Because David had a broken and contrite heart, God blessed David and Bathsheba with a second child name Solomon. God blessed David and Bathsheba's mess. Solomon became a great king.

>> **2 Samuel 7:12-13** And when thy days be fulfilled, and thou shalt sleep with thy fathers, I will set up thy seed after thee, which shall proceed out of thy bowels, and I will establish his kingdom. He shall build an house for my name, and I will stablish the throne of his kingdom for ever.

God Will Bless Your Mess

1 Corinthians 7:12-13 But to the rest speak I, not the Lord: If any brother hath a wife that believeth not, and she be pleased to dwell with him, let him not put her away. And the woman which hath an husband that believeth not, and if he be pleased to dwell with her, let her not leave him.

What this verse is showing us is the "perfect will" of God. It is God's perfect will that we marry someone who believes in His son, Jesus Christ. Remember each of us was given by God the freedom to choose to marry whomever our hearts desire. But, if you marry an unbeliever, and things "go weird" after the marriage, the Lord invites to you to return to the throne of grace to plead with him:

Isaiah 43:26 NLT Let us review the situation [your part] together, and you can present your case if you have one.

If you married an unbeliever, your present situation is a crooked way. God said, if you are called by His name, He can make any crooked way straight. Seeing restoration or reconciliation come to your covenant relationship may seem impossible for you, but your present condition is not impossible for God to heal or restore.

Are you willing to submit your will to the Lord? If you are willing to submit your will over to God's will; God will bless your mess! **Isaiah 42:16** I will make darkness light before them, and crooked things straight.

1 Corinthians 7:14 For the unbelieving husband is sanctified by the wife, and the unbelieving wife is sanctified by the husband: else were your children unclean; but now are they holy.

1 Corinthians 7:16 For what knowest thou, O wife, whether thou shalt save thy husband? or how knowest thou, O man, whether thou shalt save thy wife?

To sanctify means to be made holy. With the Holy Spirit's help, the believing spouse begins to declares those things that be not [their spouse is unsaved, or living in a backslidden state] as though they were [their spouse is reconciled into or brought back into the kingdom; and they are delivered from death, and are working out their salvation]. The believing spouse's prayers will consecrate [set a hedge of protection around] the unbelieving spouse to remind God of His promise that, **Acts 16:31** If [*you*] be saved, [*your*] whole house shall be saved.

Chapter 12

It Is Not All About You

Our entire social structure is based on marriage. God ordained the first covenant relationship - marriage. **Malachi 2:14** Yet you say, "For what reason?" Because the LORD has been witness between you and the wife of your youth,....

Parents; being married is not all about you. Marriage is about God gaining an heritage from the fruit of the marital relationship. God's gift and heritage are the children. **Psalms 127:3** Lo, children are an heritage of the Lord: and the fruit of the womb is his reward.

In a study by Michael J. McManus, he reports that children of divorce are twice as more likely to drop out of school than children from homes where the parents stayed together. Children born out of wedlock are three times more likely to have a baby out of wedlock and 12 times more likely to become involved in criminal acts or sent to jail or even prison. Another study followed 100 children for 25 years after their parent's divorce. The results indicated 60 never married, and 25 of the 60 had also divorced.[10] Another study showed if divorce distanced the parents from their children, the grandparents were also distanced from their grandchildren.[11] This sad statistic was proven to be true in my relationship with my son, and his relationship with his grandparents.

Parents, children do suffer on the sidelines watching the degrading and dysfunctional relationship between their father and mother. Children become tormented by misplaced shame if they subsequently become the product of a broken home. This statement is true for children of all ages, whether the child is five or fifty-five years old. The child or adult child is adversely affected by any perceived discord between their parents. The same goes, whether the parents separate or divorce when the child is eight or forty-eight years old. The child will be affected by the loss of their relationship with their parents. Their parent's separation or divorce will shake the very foundation of a child's love, loyalty, and their sense of security with their parents. And it will not matter whether the child is pre-school aged or the child is now a middle-aged adult.

Children may even suffer from guilt that it was their behavior that caused their parents to separate or divorce. The child may hold unresolved ill feelings towards the parent who left, and/or against the parent who stayed for years, decades, or until death. Children of divorce may carry these insecurities, unresolved anger, bitterness, or fear to trust intimacy or a person's commitment into their future relationships.

The world system tells us, "You do not have to stay in a sick, dying or dead marriage just for the children's sake". And yet in **Exodus 34:7 NLT,** God says, "I lavish unfailing love to a thousand generations. I forgive iniquity, rebellion, and sin. But I do not excuse the guilty. I lay the sins of the parents upon their children and grand-children; the entire family is affected—even children in the third and fourth generations."

Marriage is a covenant relationship. Marriage is a very serious commitment, and it is not a relationship to be entered into lightly. To be married means you are willing to be "fully" committed in your relationship with your spouse. A covenant relationship is not all about you. Husbands and wives, if you become parents, please consider your fleshly desires and ways. Do not allow the works of your flesh to become the burden your children's children will have to bear before the Lord.

Earlier in Chapter 1, I asked several core values and belief questions husbands and wives should discuss before they get married. If these core values, and beliefs or issues are not agreed upon before you marry or before you begin to have children, you are purposefully making room for the enemy to rule and reign in your covenant relationship. **Amos 3:3 NLT** Can two people walk together without agreeing on the direction?If the husband and wife are not in agreement on core values, or beliefs regarding personal or social issues, and they become parents, the children may become unintentional witnesses to this discord, and they may begin to model after their parent's behavior.

Husbands, wives, and parents, it is not all about you. It is all about Him!

Parents – You Can Draw Your Children with Loving Kindness

Children that are raised in a home or an environment where fleshly desires are apparent, learn themselves how to be rebellious. Children are amazing sponges. They were designed that way for survival sake. The child may seem to be just sitting on the floor playing with their toys, but all the while they are watching their parents. Over time, the child soon learns how to dishonor their parents. Have you ever known a time where the parents would talk inappropriately to each other in front of their children, and at the most inopportune moment, the child blurts out what they heard their parents say?America's Funniest Videos airs them all the time. The outburst may be cute and innocent on the part of the child, but oh so embarrassing for the parents. Children reflect the true habits and behaviors of their parents.

My son is the product from my first marriage. The break up of my first marriage was very turbulent. One day, my eight year old son sat witness to a fight between me and my husband. During the fight I was body slammed onto the floor, and my shoulder was dislocated. During the entire fight, my son did not make any noise, nor did he seem to respond to our raised and angry voices. I do not recall my son moving or trying to intervene when the fight turned physically violent.

Then one day when the television was tuned to America's Most Wanted; at the point where the announcer began reading the list for the ten Most Wanted people, out of the blue my son stopped playing and began to watch television. After the program was over, my son came over to me and said the oddest thing; "Wow, Mom, they did not call Dad's name."

Wow, where did my son get that idea? Then I recalled the day of that awful fight between his dad and I. Then I realized that at the time my husband and I were so caught up trying to win the "battle of who was right", we forgot about our son's need for loving parents, and a peaceful secure home. As parents, my husband and I had violated several principles in front of our son. We were disrespectful towards each other. We were verbally and physically violent towards each other in front of our son. Though our son sat quietly and obediently, I now regret that my son absorbed much more than my ex-husband and I are able to repair. We can apologize to our son for the wrong we caused, but only the Lord can heal his heart.

Parents, we are to model the Lord's commandment before our children. Our Father was so precise in creating all of us. We are His creations. The Lord says, "I knew you before I formed you in your mother's womb. **Jeremiah 1:5** God knew us before we were placed in our mother's womb. Of all the choices God had, He choose our parents for us. In **Jeremiah 3:15**, God said, "And I will give you pastors according to mine heart, which shall feed you with knowledge and understanding."

Oh, you don't think of that you are a pastor? Okay, well just for a moment let us take away the spiritual aspects of the word pastor, and let us look at the dictionary's definition for pastor[12]. A pastor is a teacher who cares for and guides a group of people. This definition is a pretty good description for "Mom" and "Dad". Parents, our Father purposefully chose us according to His heart. We were called specifically by God to feed our children knowledge and understanding. As parents, we are to raise our children in the nurture and admonition of the Lord.

Parents if you missed this point in the past know that you have been redeemed. If you are willing to admit it and quit it, with God's help, you can draw your children with loving kindness. With your hearts and minds renewed, you can move on to the next segment where you will find two major verses with supporting verses. The major verse is what God said. The supporting verses are how to settle it. Anytime you are challenged with the supporting verse go back to the major verse to hear again what God said, then work on applying the word in your heart, and then model the new behavior in front of your children.

Major verse: Luke 1:17 And he shall go before him in the spirit and power of Elias, to turn the hearts of the fathers to the children, and the disobedient to the wisdom of the just; to make ready a people prepared for the Lord.

> **Supporting verse: Ephesians 5:33** Nevertheless let every one of you in particular so love his wife even as himself; and the wife see that she reverence her husband. **Lesson Learned:** Let your children see you love and care for your spouse. Kids, whether young or old, may blush, but there isn't anything sweeter than seeing your parents in love. Gosh, after 52 years of marriage, Mom and Dad still get all "gooey-eyed" with each other. And there I am blushing and yelling like a thirteen year old, "Oh, go get a room!"

> **Supporting verse: Ephesians 3:4** And, ye fathers, provoke not your children to wrath: but bring them up in the nurture and admonition of the Lord.

Major verse: Mark 10:13-15 And they brought young children to him, that he should touch them: and his disciples rebuked those that brought them. But when Jesus saw it, he was much displeased, and said unto them, Suffer the little children to come unto me, and forbid them not: for of such is the kingdom of God. Verily I say unto you, Whosoever shall not receive the kingdom of God as a little child, he shall not enter therein.

> **Supporting verse: Proverbs 22:6** Train up a child in the way he should go: and when he is old, he will not depart from it.

> **Supporting verse: Ephesians 6:4** Fathers, do not provoke your children to anger by the way you treat them. Rather, bring them up with the discipline and

instruction that comes from the Lord. Instead: Encourage, teach, and comfort your children.

Supporting verse: Genesis 18:19 For I know him, that he will command his children and his household after him, and they shall keep the way of the Lord....

Supporting verse: 1 Corinthians 13:7 Love never gives up, never loses faith, is always hopeful, and endures through every circumstance.

Supporting verse: Acts 16:31 And they said, Believe on the Lord Jesus Christ, and thou shalt be saved, and thy house.

Parents take your children to a bible believing church, and introduce them to Jesus, God's only son.

Chapter 13

"All I Know"...For Children of Divorce

Of all of the revelations concerning the first covenant relationship, the Holy Spirit has shared with me, this chapter surprised me the most. Through my research, I found many books that talked about the children of divorce, or separation but none talked about how the Lord planned on using these children to seek and save the lost...those who are divorced, or thinking about divorce. It took me a moment, so now I pray for your patience and attention as this word unfolds. First things must be first. Children:

> **Ephesians 6:2** Honor your father and mother. This is the first of the Ten Commandments that ends with a promise: If you honor your father and mother, "you will live a long life, full of blessing."

And A Little Child Will Lead Them

> **Jeremiah 10:21** The shepherds [parents] of my people have lost their senses. They no longer seek wisdom from the LORD. Therefore, they fail completely, and their flocks are scattered.

To the children of divorce, or separation if your parents do not repent and turn back to the Lord, and you are old enough to understand the meaning of forgiveness, salvation, and covenant, the Lord wants you to know that there is a way to break the curse of parental rebellion, sin, and iniquity. The Lord would have you to know that there is even a way for a child to draw their parents with loving kindness. You can draw your parents back into the kingdom of God. Here is your example. **Isaiah 11:6** "...and a little child will lead them all".

Children – You Can Draw Your Parents with Loving Kindness

One day, a dear friend shared with me how she and her whole family came to know Jesus Christ. She told about a time when her son met her and her husband at the front door early one Sunday morning after they had been out all night partying and drinking. She told how her son insisted on going to church that very morning...he said he had to go to church that day! She said he told her he had to meet Jesus. She said she was a bit surprised, because though they did occasionally go to church, they did not attend regularly enough to be called members of any church body. She said her son insisted so much that she and the entire family got dressed and went to church that day. And it was on that very Sunday morning the whole family met the Lord. She said all of them either rededicated their life or received Jesus Christ as their Lord and Savior, and they joined that local church. Her little son led them back to the Lord and now they are all reconciled into the kingdom.

Children – You Can Break Generational Curses

Ezekiel 18:14,19-20 NLT But suppose that sinful son, in turn, has a son who sees his father's wickedness but decides against that kind of life. What? You ask. 'Doesn't the child pay for the parent's sin?' No! For the child does what is right and keeps my laws, that child will surely live. The one who sins is the one who dies. The child will not be punished for the parent's sins.

The purpose here is not for children of divorce, or separation to try to save their parent's marriage, or try to orchestrate schemes to get your parents to remarry. No, this is not your place. Your parent's made an adult decision. And as children, you do not have the right to challenge your parent's authority.

As children, we are only obligated by God's commandment to honor our parents. Honoring our parents is the first commandment that comes with a promise.

Ephesians 6:2 Honor your father and mother. This is the first of the Ten Commandments that ends with a promise: If you honor your father and mother, "you will live a long life, full of blessing."

The purpose here is to raise the awareness to children of divorce, or separation that there is a way you can break the bonds of generational curses.

Children of divorce, or separation in this next segment, you will find two major verses and supporting verses. The major verse is what God said. The supporting verses will help you to settle the word through application. Anytime you are challenged with the supporting verse go back to the major verse to hear again what God has said, then work on settling the word in your heart, and prove the word is in your life by honoring your parents by showing them the love of Christ, praying always for their reconciliation to God.

Major Verse: Matthew 10:35-39 'I have come to set a man against his father, a daughter against her mother, and a daughter-in-law against her mother-in-law. Your enemies will be right in your own household!' "If you love your father or mother more than you love me, you are not worthy of being mine; or if you love your son or daughter more than me, you are not worthy of being mine. If you refuse to take up your cross and follow me, you are not worthy of being mine. If you cling to your life, you will lose it; but if you give up your life for me, you will find it.

> **Supporting verse: Acts 16:31** And they said, Believe on the Lord Jesus Christ, and thou shalt be saved, and thy house.[13]

> **Supporting verse: Mark 3:35** Anyone who does God's will is my brother and sister and mother."

> **Supporting verse: 2 Corinthians 5:20** Now then we are ambassadors for Christ, as though God did beseech you by us; we pray you in Christ's stead, be ye reconciled to God.

Major Verse: Ezekiel 18:21-22 But if the wicked people turn away from their sins and begin to obey my laws and do what is just and right, they will surely live and not die. All their past sins will be forgotten, and they will live because of the righteous things they have done.

> **Supporting verse: Ephesians 6:2** Honor your father and mother. This is the first of the Ten Commandments that ends with a promise: If you honor your father and mother, "you will live a long life, full of blessing."

> **Supporting verse: James 5:19-20** My dear brothers and sisters, if someone (even if that someone is your

parents) among you wanders away from the truth and is brought back, you can be sure that whoever brings the sinner back will save that person from death and bring about the forgiveness of many sins.

Children of divorce, or separation, you can even break the bonds of the generational curses by doing what the Lord says is right and keeping His laws. The Lord promises if the child decides to live [to include honoring their first covenant relationship – marriage] according to His will and His purposes, that child will surely live. Children of divorce or separation you may become the very witness that draws your parents with loving kindness back into the kingdom.

A Note from my Journal
29 May 2006

I married my first husband after I found out I was pregnant with my son. My son was born in iniquity. My son and his wife are both in the Lord. Because of their love for the Lord, and their promise to remain holy until marriage, they saved themselves for each other until they married. This may seem weird, and impossible for the youth in the 21st Century, but my son and his wife allowed the Lord to help them. Father, I thank you for allowing me to see the day that you broke this generational curse.

Is There a Way to Approach My Parents? Yes, the way to approach your parents or any adult is to first respect them as an elder. With God, respecting authority is always first and foremost. Any time a junior person approaches an elder, they must always approach the elder with honor and respect.

> **1 Samuel 3:10-18** And the LORD came, and stood, and called as at other times, Samuel, Samuel. Then Samuel answered, Speak; for thy servant heareth. And the LORD said to Samuel,...I will perform against Eli all things which I have spoken concerning his house: when I begin, I will also make an end. *For I have told him that I will judge his house for ever for the iniquity which he knoweth;....* And Samuel lay until the morning, and opened the doors of the house of the LORD. *And Samuel feared to shew Eli the vision.* Then Eli called Samuel, and said, Samuel, my son. And he answered, Here am I. And he said, What is the thing that the LORD hath said unto thee? I pray thee hide it not from me: God do so to thee, and more also, if thou hide any thing from me of all the things that he said unto thee. And Samuel told him every whit, and hid nothing from him. And he said, It is the LORD: let him do what seemeth him good.

The Lord told Samuel He would judge the iniquity in Eli's house. The next morning Samuel was afraid to tell his elder, Eli, the priest what the Lord said. Samuel honored Eli so much that he would not dare disrespect Eli, even if it meant he would have to withhold from Eli what the Lord had said without first receiving Eli's permission to speak.

> Because Samuel honored his father, Samuel grew up, and the Lord was with him. **1 Samuel 3:19**

Jesus Loves the Little Children

If the children of divorce or separation are not old enough to understand the meaning of forgiveness, salvation, and covenant the Lord isn't being slow about his promise, as some people think. No, he is being patient for their sake. He does not want anyone to be destroyed, but wants everyone to repent. **2 Peter 3:9 NLT** If these children's parents are not walking according to the Word of God, are we (the body of Christ) willing to lay before the Lord until Acts 16:31 and Matthew 5:18 are made manifest for them?

> **Acts 16:31** And they said, Believe on the Lord Jesus Christ, and thou shalt be saved, and thy house.

> **Matthew 5:18** For verily I say unto you, Till heaven and earth pass, one jot or one tittle shall in no wise pass from the law, till all be fulfilled.

Once again, I have to testify of the goodness of God. If the husband/father does not respond to the call to honor the first covenant relationship, the Lord will cause the wife/mother to encompass the man. If the wife/mother does not respond to the call to honor the covenant relationship, the Lord will provide himself a lamb. **Genesis 22:8** God sent children into the earth to seek and recover the lost...those who are divorced or thinking about divorce. Let me show you an example in the Word of Truth.

> **John 9;1-3 NKJV** Now as Jesus passed by, He saw a man who was blind from birth. And his disciples asked Him, saying, "Rabbi, who sinned, this man or his parents, that he was born blind?" Jesus answered, "Neither this man nor his parents sinned, but that the works of God should be revealed.

By this account the blind man's parents did not sin, but in the case of a divorce, or separation you were born into sin and iniquity. **Psalm 51:5** Behold, I was shapen in iniquity; and in sin did my mother conceive me.

But God sent children into the earth that His works should be revealed! Wow! All this was done for one purpose. That God shall get the increase! **Psalm 127:3** Lo, children are an heritage of the LORD: and the fruit of the womb is his reward.

Now let us look up this word "heritage". Heritage means the status gained by a person through birth. God is so good to us! God receives all the glory from every birth. And God gets the glory for each child coming into the fullness of His purpose.

> **Jeremiah 1:5** Before I formed thee in the belly I knew thee; and before thou camest forth out of the womb I sanctified thee, and I ordained thee a prophet unto the nations.

Children of divorce, or separation before you came out of your mother's womb, the Lord set you apart, and ordained you to speak life into the lives of nations, your parents and through to the third and forth generations.

Children of divorce, or separation you are here on earth for a purpose. When the husband/father missed it, God called the wife. When the wife/mother missed her call, God sent a child. The Lord God called, ordained, and sent children into the earth to draw their parents with loving kindness. *This is so awesome!* Look how God established the pattern for drawing all men to Him.

> **Luke 19:9-10** And Jesus said unto him, This day is salvation come to this house, forsomuch as he also is a son of Abraham. For the Son of man is come to seek and to save that which was lost.

Children of divorce or separation, think it not robbery to be a joint with Jesus Christ. Romans 8:17 And if children, then heirs; heirs of God, and joint-heirs with Christ; if so be that we suffer with him, that we may be also glorified together. Are you willing to forgive your parents? Are you willing is to pray for your parents? If you have received Jesus Christ as your Lord and Savior, you too are an ambassador for Christ.

> **2 Corinthians 5:19-20** To wit, that God was in Christ, reconciling the world unto himself, not imputing their trespasses unto them; and hath committed unto us the word of reconciliation. Now then we are ambassadors for Christ, as though God did beseech you by us: we pray you in Christ's stead, be ye reconciled to God.

Will you be that "man" that makes up the hedge, and stands in the gap before the Lord for your parents? **Ezekiel 22:30** If you are willing, then pray:

> Father, I forgive my parents; for they know not what they do. Lord, lay not this sin to their charge. **Luke 23:34, and Acts 7:60**

And if you are willing you can be sure that whoever brings the sinner back will save that person from death and bring about the forgiveness of many sins. **James 5:20**

Children of divorce or separation you are not a mistake. God sent you into the earth for such a time as this. Having said that, here is a cautionary note:

> **Esther 4:14 Amplified** For if you keep silent at this time, relief and deliverance shall arise for the Jews (the entire body of Christ) from elsewhere, but you and your father's house shall perish. And who know but that you have come to the kingdom for such a time as this and for this very occasion.

See, the plan was right there in the Holy Bible all along! The plan was concealed in Genesis 22:8, and was revealed in Luke

19:9-10. God provided himself a lamb in the children. **Psalm 127:3** Lo, children are an heritage of the LORD: and the fruit of the womb is his reward. Children of divorce and separation, will you help recover the lost sheep of Israel?

Chapter 14

A Tale of Four Women

The next three short stories I am about to share with you are true because the Lord provided witnesses to all three accounts. The first story is about two women whose husbands died. The second story is about two divorced women. The third story is about a divorced woman and a married but separated woman. Although I write the stories in the third person, I am the first woman in all three stories, but for the privacy of the three other women and their families, their names are protected.

The Story of Two Women Whose Husbands Died

As I said, this first story is about two women whose husbands died. One Sunday after church service, the first woman sat in the church pew crying out bitter tears, when the second woman came up and touched the first woman and lifted her chin to cause her to look up. The first woman paused for a moment as the second woman peered down at the first woman with kind, and gentle eyes. Why are you crying the second woman asked? The first woman answered, 'My husband divorced me'.

Without a word the second women shined a tender smile, and give the first woman the warmest most secure hug ever. Through her tears the first woman finally recognized the second woman. She was the woman whose husband had died, and was buried the week before. "Oh Father", the first woman cried out. "Please forgive me. I am crying as if I have no hope. The second woman's husband died a physical death. My husband still has breath in his body. You have already given me the revelation into the Restoration of the First Covenant Relationship. I understand now. He is only dead to Christ."

On 28 March 2006, when the first woman's husband sought out his salvation in Christ Jesus, she received her husband back from the dead. **Hebrews 11:35** Women received their dead raised to life again....:

The Story of Two Divorced Women

This second story is about two divorced women who were given time and opportunity to pray for their husbands who chose to leave their wife, or the husbands forced the end of their marriage. Each woman was asked by the Holy Spirit to pray for their husband. Both women were asked to pray that the enemy would not come in and utterly destroy their husbands.

Though the first woman did not understand the fullness behind the revelation of the restoration of the first covenant relationship, she believed God. The first woman forgave her husband, and prayed for him to be reconciled into the kingdom.

On a cold and windy day, the Lord set up a divine appointment. On that morning, the first woman noticed the second woman waiting at a bus stop. The first woman asked the second woman if she wanted a ride, and the second woman said "Yes". While riding together, the second woman began talking about her life's current events. She began to share that she and her husband had recently divorced. The first woman realized she was given an opportunity to share with the second woman what the Holy Spirit told her concerning the restoration of the first covenant relationship. The second woman heard the testimony of the first covenant relationship, but the second woman's heart was hardened against her husband. The second woman could only recall the hurtful and seemingly unforgivable things her husband had done to her during their marriage. The second woman refused to forgive or pray for her husband. The thief came immediately and stole the second woman's seed, her prayers.

The first woman prayed for four years for her husband to be reconciled back into the kingdom. One month into the fourth year, the first woman received the good news that her husband was seeking out his salvation in Christ. The first woman's husband has joined a local church, and has an active role in that church body.

Four months after the first woman met the second woman and shared the revelation into first covenant relationship; the first woman received some very sad news. The second woman's ex-husband had died.

Now I can not provide any more of an explanation to this coincidence, other than to say this testimony is a true. God provided His witnesses. All I know is prayer does work. All I know is forgiveness will set you free, and forgiveness will free those who trespasss against you too.

Job 42:8 NLT *"Now take seven young bulls and seven rams and to my servant Job and offer a burnt offering for yourselves. My servant Job will pray for you, and I will accept his prayer on your behalf. I will not treat you as you deserve,..."*

The Story of the Divorced Woman, and a Married but Separated Woman

This third story is about a divorced woman, and a married but separated woman. The first woman is presently healthy, and the Lord is truly sustaining her. As a husband, the Lord provides for the first woman's every need.

The first woman desires with all her heart to be again what she is called to be...a wife. The first woman often pleads before the Lord for the restoration of the first covenant relationship. One day, the Lord asked the first woman, "Am I not better to you than ten husbands?" In her mind, the first woman thought to herself, "No. Father, you said it is not good for man to be alone, and I am found alone." And the Lord knew the first woman's thoughts.

The second woman, though married, she and her husband are living separately. The second woman has biblical basis to divorce her husband, however she choose to remain married, albeit she did separate from her husband. The second woman suffered through the separation from her spouse. But she soon found comfort, love, joy, and peace in the arms of the Lord.

The second woman's health deteriorated and caused her to become home bound. Because of the state of her health, the second woman requires daily personal care and assistance. When the second woman's husband came to himself, he realized that he had made a mistake in leaving his wife, and his marriage, that he made a quality decision to return to his wife. Today, he is very attentive to his wife. He meets her every need. The second woman's husband is even sustaining her business concerns until her health recovers. Oh, you should see how tender he is with her.

And yet, the second woman found herself resenting her husband for coming between her and her Lord. One day in conversation, the second woman began to vent to the first woman how she wished she had things back the way they were when it was just her and her Lord.

The second woman's venting grieved the first woman. The first woman said, "please, do not despise your husband for wanting to come back to you. Don't you know that the Lord has truly blessed you by turning the heart of your husband back to you? Can't you see the Lord knew that in your present condition, you would need the covering, extra care, and comfort only an earthly husband could bring. Please receive your blessing with a glad heart." Then the first woman shared the revelation of the restoration of the first covenant relationship with the second woman. After hearing the testimony, the second woman realized how truly blessed of the Lord she really was. We are very good friends to this day.

Epilogue

In closing, I am steadfast in my purpose. My assignment was to tell you what I have heard and seen concerning the restoration of the first covenant relationship – marriage. All I know is lives have been changed. All I know is hearts and minds are being reconciled back to the Father. All I know is husbands and wives are reaffirming their commitment to each other. And all I know is the hearts of fathers are turning back to their children. All I know is all these things bring glory of God.

> **Luke 4:18-19** The Spirit of the Lord is upon me, because he hath anointed me to preach the gospel to the poor; he has sent me to heal the brokenhearted, to preach deliverance to the captives, and to recover the sight to the blind to set at liberty them that are bruised. To preach the acceptable year of the Lord.

If I may be so bold to make this verse personal; the Spirit of the LORD is upon me, for he has anointed me to tell you the Good News concerning the restoration of the first covenant relationship – marriage. To this vision I am fully persuaded and committed.

Our Father loves us with an everlasting love. With loving kindness He drew us to Him. When the Lord gave us His son, Jesus Christ, He showed us His blueprint for restoring the first covenant relationship. The pattern for the restoration of the first covenant relationship was drawn with loving kindness.

Chapter 15

Salvation Is Available To Everyone

As I said before, I used to pray to God to help me when I was troubled or distressed. But at that time in my life, the Lord, He did not know me as His child. I believed that I was a good person, and the Lord would hear and help me. I thought because I was basically a good person, the Lord would answer my prayers.

But I was unsaved. I was out of reach of His protection, grace and mercy. God was not under any obligation to help me or answer my prayers. Yes, the Lord knew me; He created me. Yes, the Lord loved me. He knew me before I was in my mother's womb. But I was not His own. I had not yet professed the name of Jesus. I had not accepted Jesus as God's only son, given for my salvation. At that time in my life I was lost, in a dead state because He never knew me.

> **Matthew 7:21-23** Not every one that saith unto me, Lord, Lord, shall enter into the kingdom of heaven; but the that doeth the will of my Father which is in heaven. Many will say to me that day, Lord, Lord, have we not prophesied in thy name? and in thy name have cast out devils? and in thy name done many wonderful works? And then will I profess unto them, I never knew you: depart from me, ye that work iniquity.

You too can walk in the Lord's protection and have full rights to His provisions. In order to receive the benefits of having direct access to the Father, you first need to receive Jesus Christ as your Lord and Savior. All you need to do to receive Jesus Christ as your Lord and Savior you can find in:

Romans 10:9-13 NLT If you confess with your mouth that Jesus is Lord and believe in your heart that God raised him from the dead, you will be saved. For it is by believing in your heart that you are made right with God, and it is by confessing with your mouth that you are saved. As the Holy Scriptures tell us, "Anyone who trusts in him will never be disgraced." Jew and Gentile are the same in this respect. They have the same Lord, who gives generously to all who call on him. For "Everyone who calls on the name of the Lord will be saved."

1. Confess with your mouth that Jesus Christ is Lord.
2. Believe in your heart God raised Jesus from the dead and you will be saved.
3. Anyone who calls on the name of the Lord will be saved.

Prayer For Salvation

Holy Father, in Jesus' name, please forgive me of my sins and cleanse me of mine iniquities. Come into my heart, wash me and make me clean. Father, I thank you for sending your son Jesus to die on the cross for my sins. Father, I believe in my heart that you raised Jesus Christ from the dead. Father, I need your son Jesus to come into my life to be my Lord and savior. In Jesus' name. Amen.

How Do I Know That I Am Saved?

1 John 2:3,5-6 NLT And how can we be sure that we belong to him? By obeying his commandments. But those who obey God's word really do love him. That is the way to know whether or we live in him. Those who say they live in God should live their lives as Christ did.

How Do I Know That God Will Hear Me?

1 John 5:14-15 NLT And we can be confident that he will listen to us whenever we ask him for anything in line with his will. And if we know that he is listening when we make our requests, we can be sure that he will give us what we ask for.

Acknowledgements

First, I give honor to the Father, for He is the head of my life. I thank the Lord for sending His son Jesus to be my savior. I thank Jesus Christ for giving me the gift of the Holy Spirit, for without the Holy Spirit's teachings this book would still be blank sheets of paper. Father, thank you for giving me pastors who fed me with knowledge and understanding. Pastor Charles Barlow ministered to me at the alter and ushered me into the kingdom. Pastor Tobitha Lawrence nurtured me as a babe in Christ. Apostle Leon Brown released me to my spiritual father. Father, I thank you for giving me a spiritual father, Prophet Rodney S. Walker, Sr. who launched me into my destiny. I thank God for my parents, Mr. Albert and Mrs. Annie Mae Roberson, grown as I am I know I am still be their baby girl. To my three sisters and my brother, you heard this story first and each of you in your own way gave me your unconditional support. To my son Byron and his wife Jennifer, I am so very proud of you. A special thanks to Mrs. Octavia M. Cotton for undeniable wisdom that will resonate in 21st Century ears and beyond. A special thanks to Lorence and Sarita Williams of LS Techniq for producing another excellent book cover. To my Christian brother and sisters of good report, Mr. Eric and Mrs. Angela Jones, and Mrs. Phyllis Brantley, you were made a witness on purpose to this testimony. To Kenneth O. Dallas Sr. all I know concerning you...the half has not been told.

Notes

[1] Galatians 4:29 *Amplified Bible* Yet [just] as at that time the child [of ordinary birth] born according to the flesh despised and persecuted him [who was born remarkably] according to [the promise and the working of] the [Holy] Spirit, so it is now also.

[2] 2 Chronicles 7:14 If my people, which are called by my name, shall humble themselves, and pray, and seek my face, and turn from their wicked ways; then will I hear from heaven, and will forgive their sin, and will heal their land.

[3] Core values or beliefs are those that if someone violated them, or infringed on your boundaries you would object, or violently reject their action or behavior.

[4] http://www.barna.org

[5] Added for clarity.

[6] Salvation is available to everyone. See Romans 10:9-13 or Chapter 15.

[7] Salvation is available to everyone. See Romans 10:9-13 or Chapter 15.

[8] Italics are for emphasis only.

[9] Prayer of Salvation - See Chapter 15

[10] *Mutual Consent Divorce Reform* by Michael J. McManus, Sept. 14, 2004 Column #1,203

[11] "Generations of love evolve from divorce" by Amy Harmon in *The New York Times* March 23, 2005

[12] *Webster's II New Riverside University Dictionary*, 1988

[13] Salvation is available to everyone. See Romans 10:9-13 or Chapter 15.